BARRON'S BOOK NOTES

WILLIAM GOLDING'S
Lord of the Flies

BY

W. Meitcke

SERIES EDITOR

Michael Spring
Editor, *Literary Cavalcade*
Scholastic Inc.

BARRON'S

BARRON'S EDUCATIONAL SERIES, INC.

ACKNOWLEDGMENTS

We would like to acknowledge the many painstaking hours of work Holly Hughes and Thomas F. Hirsch have devoted to make the *Book Notes* series a success.

All inquiries should be addressed to:
Barron's Educational Series, Inc.
250 Wireless Boulevard
Hauppauge, New York 11788

Library of Congress Catalog Card No. 84-18504

International Standard Book No. 0-8120-3426-0

Library of Congress Cataloging in Publication Data

William Golding's Lord of the flies.

(Barron's book notes)
Bibliography: p. 96
Summary: A guide to reading "Lord of the Flies" with
a critical and appreciative mind. Includes background on
the author's life and times, sample tests, term paper
suggestions, and a reading list.
    1. Golding, William, 1911–   . Lord of the flies.
[1. Golding, William, 1911–   . Lord of the flies.
2. English literature—History and criticism] I. Title.
PR6013.035L645   1984   823'.914   84-18504
ISBN 0-8120-3426-0 (pbk.)

PRINTED IN THE UNITED STATES OF AMERICA

3   550   98765

CONTENTS

Advisory Board   v

How to Use This Book   vii

THE AUTHOR AND HIS TIMES   1

THE NOVEL   5

The Plot   5

The Characters   9

Other Elements   17

    Setting   17

    Themes   18

    Style   20

    Point of View   22

    Structure   23

The Story   25

A STEP BEYOND   85

Tests and Answers   85

Term Paper Ideas   93

Further Reading   96

    Critical Works   96

    Author's Other Works   96

The Critics   98

HOW TO USE THIS BOOK

You have to know how to approach literature in order to get the most out of it. This *Barron's Book Notes* volume follows a plan based on methods used by some of the best students to read a work of literature.

Begin with the guide's section on the author's life and times. As you read, try to form a clear picture of the author's personality, circumstances, and motives for writing the work. This background usually will make it easier for you to hear the author's tone of voice, and follow where the author is heading.

Then go over the rest of the introductory material—such sections as those on the plot, characters, setting, themes, and style of the work. Underline, or write down in your notebook, particular things to watch for, such as contrasts between characters and repeated literary devices. At this point, you may want to develop a system of symbols to use in marking your text as you read. (Of course, you should only mark up a book you own, not one that belongs to another person or a school.) Perhaps you will want to use a different letter for each character's name, a different number for each major theme of the book, a different color for each important symbol or literary device. Be prepared to mark up the pages of your book as you read. Put your marks in the margins so you can find them again easily.

Now comes the moment you've been waiting for—the time to start reading the work of literature. You may want to put aside your *Barron's Book Notes* volume until you've read the work all the way through. Or you may want to alternate, reading the *Book Notes* analysis of each section as soon as you have finished reading the corresponding part of the original. Before you move on, reread crucial passages you don't fully understand. (Don't take this guide's analysis for granted—make up your own mind as to what the work means.)

Once you've finished the whole work of literature, you may want to review it right away, so you can firm up your ideas about what it means. You may want to leaf through the book concentrating on passages you marked in reference to one character or one theme. This is also a good time to reread the *Book Notes* introductory material, which pulls together insights on specific topics.

When it comes time to prepare for a test or to write a paper, you'll already have formed ideas about the work. You'll be able to go back through it, refreshing your memory as to the author's exact words and perspective, so that you can support your opinions with evidence drawn straight from the work. Patterns will emerge, and ideas will fall into place; your essay question or term paper will almost write itself. Give yourself a dry run with one of the sample tests in the guide. These tests present both multiple-choice and essay questions. An accompanying section gives answers to the multiple-choice questions as well as suggestions for writing the essays. If you have to select a term paper topic, you may choose one from the list of suggestions in this book. This guide also provides you with a reading list, to help you when you start research for a term paper, and a selection of provocative comments by critics, to spark your thinking before you write.

THE AUTHOR AND HIS TIMES

William Golding was born in 1911 and grew up in the years before World War II. That war changed thinking about man's essential nature. Before the war people generally believed that man was essentially good-hearted and society often was evil. However, the atrocities of the war made it impossible for many people to believe any longer in man's basic innocence. You can see the influence of this shift in thinking in Golding's works.

Some of Golding's favorite childhood authors were Edgar Rice Burroughs (*Tarzan of the Apes*), Robert Ballantyne (*Coral Island*), and Jules Verne (*Twenty Thousand Leagues Under the Sea*). Each of these books portrays man as a basically good creature who struggles to avoid the evils of society.

Golding yearned to be like the characters in the fables and stories he read. The island setting for *Lord of the Flies* and the names Ralph, Jack, and Simon have been taken from *Coral Island*. "They held me rapt," Golding once said of the books he read. "I dived with the *Nautilus*, was shot round the moon, crossed Darkest Africa in a balloon, descended to the center of the earth, drifted in the South Atlantic, dying of thirst. . . . It always sent me indoors for a drink—the fresh waters of the Amazon."

At about the age of twelve Golding decided to be a writer. He planned a twelve-volume work on trade unions but could never complete the enormous undertaking. With his love of reading and his early

attempts at writing, Golding of course studied literature in college.

When World War II began in 1939, Golding joined
the Royal Navy. He saw action against German war-
ships, he was in antisubmarine and antiaircraft oper-
ations, and in 1944 he was involved in the D-Day
naval support for the landings on the beaches of Nor-
mandy. He continued to read the classics even as he
acquired a reputation for loving tense combat. And
his war experiences changed his view about mankind's essential nature. Because of the atrocities he
witnessed, Golding came to believe that there was a
very dark and evil side to man. "The war," he said,
"was unlike any other fought in Europe. It taught us
not fighting, politics or the follies of nationalism, but
about the given nature of man."

After the war Golding returned to teaching in a
boys' school, which may explain why the characters
in *Lord of the Flies* seem so real. Ralph, Jack, Piggy,
Simon, and the other boys are based on the faces and
voices of children Golding knew. Thus his reading of
the classics, his war experience, and his new insight
into humanity laid the groundwork for his writing.

His first three novels were very much like novels he
had read, and he called them the "rubbish" of imita-
tion. They have never been published. His fourth
novel was *Lord of the Flies*, and when it was finally
accepted for publication in 1954, it had been turned
down by more than twenty publishers.

The book was not considered a success at first. It
was not until the 1960s, when it had captured the
imaginations of college and high school students, that
critics began to acknowledge Golding's talent. Even
now there are differing opinions about the novel.
Some believe Golding's writing is bombastic and
didactic, that he does not allow you to have any opin-

ion but his. Other critics see him as the greatest English writer of our time. You will find that part of the fun of his book lies in deciding for yourself what you think.

Golding has continued to write in spite of the controversy over his work. It would seem that the criticism, rather than frightening him, only challenges him to continue writing. In the same way, Golding challenges readers to think about what he considers most important: the true nature of human beings.

The three novels that followed *Lord of the Flies*—*The Inheritors, Pincher Martin,* and *Free Fall*—brought him more success, while the controversy over his talent, or lack of it, continued. Eventually Golding stopped teaching to write full time. In 1983 Golding was awarded the Nobel Prize for Literature, which is given a writer not for one particular volume but for the body of his work. This was the recognition and respect that many believe he had deserved all along.

THE NOVEL

The Plot

A group of boys has been dropped on a tropical island somewhere in the Pacific Ocean, their plane having been shot down. A nuclear war has taken place; civilization has been destroyed.

Ralph, a strong and likable blond, delights in the fact that there are "no grownups" around to supervise them. The boys have the entire island to themselves.

Piggy, who is fat, asthmatic, and nearly blind without his glasses, trails behind as Ralph explores the island. When they find a white conch shell, Piggy encourages Ralph to blow on it. Ralph sounds the conch and the other boys appear.

Among them is Jack Merridew, marching the boys' choir, military style, in the blazing sun. There are also the twins, Sam and Eric. Simon, short and skinny with black hair, joins the group. Many other boys who are never given names straggle in.

The group elects Ralph as their leader even though Jack would like to be chosen. Ralph, Simon, and Jack explore the island. It's hard for them to believe they're really on their own, but once they're convinced, Jack decides to be the hunter and provide food. A first attempt at killing a piglet fails.

When the conch calls the group together again, they talk about the need for hunters. A small boy with a mulberry-colored birthmark on his face says he is afraid of a snakelike beast in the woods. Is there really such a beast? The boys can't agree. However, the fear of the beast, of the dark, and of what is unknown about the island is very real and an important part of the story. Ralph convinces everyone that they need a fire for a signal in case a ship passes the island.

Starting a fire is impossible until they use Piggy's glasses. Then the boys often abandon the fire to play, finding it hard work keeping the fire going.

Jack becomes more and more obsessed with hunting and the desire to kill. He says that "you can feel as if you're not hunting, but—being hunted, as if something's behind you all the time in the jungle." Jack and his hunters paint their faces to look like masks. Hiding behind the masks, they are able to slaughter a pig. Afterward Jack and the hunters reenact the killing, one of the boys pretending to be the pig.

Again the fear of the beast is mentioned, and the littlest boys cry about their nightmares while the big ones fight about the existence of the beast. Simon says that perhaps the beast is "only us," but the others laugh him down. Their fears mushroom when the twins, Sam and Eric, see something that does indeed look like the beast. Jack and Ralph lead an exploration and come back convinced there is a beast. Jack decides he no longer wants to be part of Ralph's tribe. He leaves, inviting the other boys to follow him.

In spite of their growing terror, Jack leads the hunters into the jungle for the slaying of another pig. He places its head on a stake, much like a primitive offering to the unknown beast. Everyone but the twins and Piggy abandon Ralph to attend Jack's feast of roast pig.

Alone in the woods, Simon has a seizure and talks to the pig's head on the stake. In Simon's hallucination the head becomes the Lord of the Flies and says, "Fancy thinking the Beast was something you could hunt and kill! You knew, didn't you? I'm part of you?"

A great storm builds over the island, and Simon starts back to where the other boys are. As he stumbles through the jungle, he discovers the beast that the twins thought they saw. A dead man who had parachuted from his plane is caught on the rocks. Terrified and sickened by the sight, Simon loosens the lines and frees the dead man, then starts off to tell the others there is no beast.

In the meantime, Ralph has given in and joined Jack's feast; Piggy and the twins follow. They share roast pig and find that the hunters are now treating Jack as a god, serving him and obeying his commands. Ralph and Jack argue over who should be leader. Jack claims the right because he has killed the pig, but Ralph still has the conch. Instead of fighting, Jack suggests they do their pig-killing dance. They begin to chant, "Kill the beast! Cut his throat! Spill his blood!" as the storm overhead gathers force. Piggy and Ralph join the circle to dance with the others. Lightning cuts the sky apart.

When Simon appears, the boys have ceased to be boys playing a game and have become a dangerous mob. They attack Simon, calling him the beast and killing him with their hunting sticks. Only then does the storm finally break and the rain begin to fall. During the night the tide carries the dead boy out to sea.

The next night Jack and two hunters attack Ralph and Piggy and steal Piggy's glasses. Nearly blind without his glasses, Piggy decides that he and Ralph can do nothing but ask Jack to give them back. Sam and Eric, the only others who have remained with Ralph, go along. They take the conch with them.

The fight that has been building between Jack and Ralph over who should be leader finally breaks out. The hunters drag the twins off. A giant boulder is hurled over a ledge , demolishing the conch and strik-ing Piggy. Flung over the cliff, Piggy dies when he hits the rocks below. Jack declares himself chief.

The next day Jack and the hunters plan to cover the island looking for Ralph. He will be stalked in much the same way that Jack has gone after the pigs. Ralph hides and runs, becoming more and more a cornered animal. To smoke him out, a fire is started that quickly spreads over the island.

At the very last moment, when all hope for him seems lost, Ralph stumbles onto the beach and falls at the feet of a man in uniform. Ralph is saved.

While the officer is disappointed at how poorly the boys have managed themselves on the island, Ralph can only weep "for the end of innocence, the dark-ness of man's heart, and the fall through the air of the true, wise friend called Piggy."

The Characters

William Golding has chosen the names of his characters with special care. You will notice that in most cases the root meaning of a name is related to the personality of the character.

Ralph

Ralph, originally from the Anglo-Saxon language, means "counsel." Ralph holds group meetings to share his power as leader.

Ralph, a blond boy of twelve, is the first character you meet. Golding says he is strong like a boxer and quite handsome. He is likable from the start. He turns cartwheels in the sand when he realizes there are no grownups on the island, and before enjoying his first swim in the lagoon he drops his clothing about the jungle as if it were his bedroom. Ralph is like Adam in the garden of Eden, like a child left alone to play his favorite games.

His most distinguishing characteristic is his strong belief that someone will come to rescue the boys. Initially he is so assured of this that he doesn't worry about their situation. Later he insists the boys keep a fire going as a signal to passing boats. Ralph's clinging to his belief establishes the conflict in the story between himself and Jack.

Ralph is not as thoughtful or as questioning as Piggy, not as spiritual as Simon or as aggressive as Jack. There is something good-natured about Ralph; he reminds us of someone we know or would want to know.

Ralph shows fairness when he tries to share leadership of the boys with Jack, and he shows common sense in establishing rules to run the assemblies.

Ralph is an embodiment of democracy; he is willing to be a leader but knows that it's important for each of the boys to be able to speak his mind. When there is a decision to be made, he lets the boys vote on it.

Even when the boys do not live up to the responsibilities they've agreed on, Ralph does not use punishment to get them to do what he believes is right. Instead he tries to talk sensibly to them. You might consider Ralph a strong person who doesn't want to use force as a method to get things done on the island. On the other hand, Ralph could be called stupid for not using force to take control of the boys in an extreme situation. (Depending on your own beliefs, you may find yourself siding with the attitudes of some of the important characters.)

Ralph undergoes a profound change of personality during the island stay. Because of Jack's aggressiveness, the fear of the beast, and his own insistence on a signal fire, Ralph begins to grapple with the problems of being a leader. The playful part of his nature is lost as he begins to recognize that he does not have Piggy's skill for thinking. Unsuccessfully, he tries to ponder the boys' fears and to act like an adult. He becomes more considerate of others as his self-awareness grows.

Ralph can be said to represent the all-around, basically good person. He is not perfect, but he recognizes the need for responsibility, and he takes it on even though he is not particularly skilled at it.

Jack

Jack comes from the Hebrew and means "one who supplants," one who takes over by force. This is how Jack gains and uses power. He is the character who has the most conflict with Ralph.

the strange things he says. He is friends with no one in particular, and no one really befriends him. Even though he is willing to help build shelters with Ralph, he often disappears on his own.

The reason Simon may be a loner is that he has a disability which makes him slightly different from the other boys: Simon has epilepsy.

In ancient times many thought that the epileptic seizure was an indication that a person had great spiritual powers and was favored by communications from the gods. In an ironic twist, Simon communicates with an evil figure rather than a loving god. He is the only boy who hears the Lord of the Flies speak and learns that the beast is within himself rather than in the jungle.

Because of his spiritual nature, he understands what most boys his age never think about. Simon alone knows for certain that there is no such thing as a beast, that there is only the fear that is inside each boy. He knows that this is what terrifies them. It terrifies him also, and it makes him unable to talk about it. That is why, when he does speak, the words come out so strangely.

Simon is the most compassionate of the boys; he is like a priest or a saint—exactly the opposite of Jack. When Simon sees the dead man in the parachute, he frees him in spite of the horror he feels.

What Simon knows makes him unable to become a savage like the hunters or Jack. He can't even defend himself at the moment of his own slaughter. And when he tries to tell the boys what they cannot understand, they make him the beast of their fears. He is killed by the strength of their belief in the beast.

Simon is one of the most important characters because the story revolves around fear of the beast and he is the only boy who confronts it, during one of his seizures. He hears the truth, and in spite of the consequences he tells it.

Simon's spiritual power is invisible and personal. Someone like Jack, who has no internal understanding or respect for such things, can easily destroy Simon, but he can't destroy Simon's spiritual power. This power is also misunderstood by Ralph, who can't figure out the problem of the beast. Simon's ability is never recognized by his peers.

You will want to consider what Golding is saying about the Simons of the world. They are doomed to die because of what they know and their inability to talk about it. Yet they are the most noble of people because of their willingness to try.

Piggy

Piggy has an obvious meaning, and the name connects the boy to the pigs which the other boys hunt and kill.

Piggy is a little like Simon in that he is the butt of cruelty and laughter. He has several disabilities—his asthma, his obesity, and his near blindness—and they set him apart from the other boys. But his illnesses have isolated him and given him time to think about life. Like Simon, Piggy is wiser than most of the boys; however, he is able to speak up at meetings more than Simon can, and he becomes Ralph's respected friend.

As advisor to Ralph, Piggy understands more than Ralph does. It is Piggy who knows that blowing the conch will call the boys together. Piggy tries to help Ralph keep order. He also tries to think what adults would do if they were in the same situation. Piggy represents civilization and its hold on man.

Piggy is a thinking person, one who has a strong belief in scientific explanations and rational solutions to problems. However, Piggy has his blind spots. He wants to believe that once you're an adult, you no longer fear the dark, and that life can always be explained. He also wants little to do with understanding evil. After Simon has been murdered, Piggy tries to deny and rationalize the killing.

Piggy's presence on the island is a constant reminder of how thinking people live. In the jungle he becomes weakened, civilization recedes, and with his death the law of the jungle prevails. Piggy is Golding's argument for the need of civilization and his case against man's return to a more innocent state in nature.

Roger

Roger comes from the German and means "spear." Roger's power is the use of brute force totally at whim.

As Jack's right-hand man, Roger darkly parallels Piggy's relationship to Ralph. There is much conversation between Piggy and Ralph but little between Jack and Roger. Roger carries out, to an extreme, Jack's aggressive use of force. Roger's brute force is indiscriminate.

Roger is the cruelest of the characters, and even though he doesn't play a large part in the story, his role leaves the reader shuddering. Roger uses his spear to torment the sow after the boys have captured it. Later he brags about it, flaunting his meanness. He is responsible for wantonly murdering Piggy, using a stick to pry loose a boulder that bounds down and strikes him.

Roger represents the worst that develops in people when there is no civilization to keep them in line. Roger despises civilization and sees it as a hindrance to what he wants.

Sam and Eric

Sam and Eric are twins who are incapable of acting independently of one another. They seem to become one person, answering to a name that has been slurred together into Samneric. They represent loss of identity through fear of the beast.

Other Elements

SETTING

The story takes place on an island in the ocean, an island the author never actually locates in the real world. He does this so that you can imagine most of the island in your own way. You might even want to draw a map of the island, locating on it all the features listed below (the underlined words). You will be exploring and getting to know the island in the same way that the boys have to, that is, little by little. If you include each of the sections, you will be able to follow the story more closely. A map will also let you experience how terribly trapped Ralph must have felt when he was being stalked by Jack.

The author tells us that the island is tropical and shaped like a boat. At the low end are the jungle and the orchards, which rise up to the treeless and rocky mountain ridge.

The beach near the warm water lagoon is where Piggy and Ralph first talk and find the conch. This is also where they hold their meetings. The author calls it a "natural platform of fallen trees."

Not far away is the fruit orchard where the boys can eat all they want and Ralph complains when the boys are "taken short."

Inland from the lagoon is the jungle with pig trails and hanging vines which the "littluns" fear. Here Jack hunts the pigs, and then Ralph, and this is where the beast supposedly lives. The jungle is also Simon's hiding place when he goes to see the candle bushes. In the same area he sees the pig's head that Jack mounted on a stake.

The island has a <u>mountain</u> that Ralph, Simon, and Jack climb, and from which they are able to see the terrain. This is where the boys are supposed to keep a fire going and where the parachutist landed on the rocks.

Finally, there is the <u>castle</u> at the other end of the island, which rises a hundred feet above the sea. This is where the first search for the beast is made. It becomes Jack's headquarters when he declares himself chief, and it is from the castle that Piggy falls to his death on the rocks below.

Golding gives us a very strong sense of place, and the island shapes the story's direction. At the outset the boys view it as a paradise; it is lush and abundant with food. As the fear of the beast grows, it becomes a hell in which fire and fear prevail.

The island setting works as a metaphor for the world. The boys are trapped on the island as we are trapped on this planet. What happens there becomes a commentary on our world. The island is also described as a boat, and the boys feel they are men about to embark on an adventure. When the story closes, a boat has landed on the island. The boys' first adventure is over, but they are about to begin another.

THEMES

Theme is the underlying truth of the story, not the plot but what the plot means. In *Lord of the Flies* there are many themes, and they are interwoven with each other.

1. THE NEED FOR CIVILIZATION
The most obvious of the themes is man's need for civilization. Contrary to the belief that man is innocent and society evil, the story shows that laws and rules,

policemen and schools are necessary to keep the darker side of human nature in line. When these institutions and concepts slip away or are ignored, human beings revert to a more primitive part of their nature.

2. INNOCENCE AND THE LOSS OF IT

The existence of civilization allows man to remain innocent or ignorant about his true nature. Although man needs civilization, it is important that he also be aware of his more primitive instincts. Only in this way can he reach true maturity.

Golding implies that the loss of innocence has little to do with age but is related to a person's understanding of human nature. It can happen at any age or not at all. Painful though it may be, this loss of innocence by coming to terms with reality is necessary if humanity is to survive.

3. THE LOSS OF IDENTITY

Civilization separates man from the animals by teaching him to think and make choices. When civilization slips away and man reverts to his more primitive nature, his identity disintegrates. The boys use masks to cover their identity, and this allows them to kill and later to murder. The loss of a personal name personifies the loss of selfhood and identity.

4. POWER

Different types of power, with their uses and abuses, are central to the story. Each kind of power is used by one of the characters. Democratic power is shown when choices and decisions are shared among many. Authoritarian power allows one person to rule by threatening and terrifying others. Spiritual power recognizes internal and external realities and attempts to integrate them. Brute force, the most primitive use of power, is indiscriminate.

5. FEAR OF THE UNKNOWN

Fear of the unknown on the island revolves around the boys' terror of the beast. Fear is allowed to grow because they play with the idea of it. They cannot fully accept the notion of a beast, nor can they let go of it. They whip themselves into hysteria, and their attempts to resolve their fears are too feeble to convince themselves one way or the other. The recognition that no real beast exists, that there is only the power of fear, is one of the deepest meanings of the story.

6. THE INDIFFERENCE OF NATURE

Throughout much of literature the natural world has been portrayed as "mother nature," the protector of man. In *Lord of the Flies* nature is shown to be indifferent to humanity's existence. When nature creates a situation which helps or hinders mankind, it is an arbitrary happening. Man may be aware of nature, but nature is unconscious and unaware of mankind.

7. BLINDNESS AND SIGHT

Being blind and having special sight are interwoven themes. One who is blind to his immediate surroundings usually has special understanding of things which others cannot fathom. This person sees more, but he is not seen or recognized by those around him. Such a person is often considered a fool and ridiculed by others.

STYLE

Although the story is exciting and fast-moving, the style of writing is a deliberate one. In order to write such a compelling novel, Golding needed to be very much in control of his material. The story can be overwhelming for us, but he had to be objective about it in order to mold it as he did.

You can see instances of his ability to make us feel a certain way in the length and kinds of sentences he uses. When he wants the action to move slowly, he uses long, deliberate sentences that slow the reader's pace, making us feel as though we too are having a leisurely time. Note the beginning of Chapter 4, when the boys have been on the island awhile: "The first rhythm that they became used to was the slow swing from dawn to quick dusk. They accepted the pleasures of morning, the bright sun, the whelming sea and sweet air, as a time when play was good and life so full that hope was not necessary and therefore forgotten." That long, graceful sentence is intended to give us a feeling for the slow passage of time and the leisurely way in which the boys spent their mornings.

When Ralph is being stalked by the boys at the climax, we feel his anxiety. Notice the short, choppy sentences that can be read quickly and that give a sensation of running. Notice also the brevity of Ralph's thoughts, as if there isn't much time to think. "Break the line. A tree. Hide, and let them pass. . . . Hide was better than a tree because you had a chance of breaking the line if you were discovered. Hide then."

There is also Golding's deliberate choice of words. We've seen how each character's name represents an essential aspect of his personality. On the opening page Golding gives a sense of the jungle's menace in spite of the fact that Ralph thinks it's a paradise. The choice of words gives us the clue. Piggy and Ralph are both scratched by "thorns." Piggy is trapped in the "creepers." Golding lets us know before the characters do that this isn't a friendly place.

The use of emotional material is also greatly controlled. Golding shows no sentimentality about Piggy's death as he gives the gruesome details of Piggy's twitching on the rocks.

The deliberate use of imagery enhances the meaning of the story by appealing to the senses. Simon's meditation is surrounded by butterflies, and the Lord of the Flies is covered by flies. Birds make witchlike cries, and coconuts are described as skulls.

Golding also uses a mirroring technique. At the opening of the story, when the boys explore the island, they are excited with what they find. Here the description is filled with light, color, and friendship. The second exploration recalls the first, but the boys have become leery of one another. They are searching for the beast; there are gloom, fear, and isolation in the description.

POINT OF VIEW

In *Lord of the Flies* the point of view shifts several times. For most of the story we see events through the eyes of the boys. Sometimes it is through Ralph's eyes that we watch, at other times through Piggy's or Simon's. We are on the island with them, and we are close to what is happening to them.

However, sometimes the author steps into the story to give information that is not in the realm of the boys' experience. When the parachutist lands on the island, the author tells about the war that is still going on in the world. There are also the descriptions of the mirages in nature and the sea's dragging Simon's body away.

At the close of the story, when we are close to what is happening to Ralph, the author again backs us away from it. He turns us around, and we find we are seeing the boys through the eyes of the officer. Golding does this deliberately. By making us feel what Ralph is experiencing and thinking, Golding forces us to get caught up in the story and forget about being objective. Then, bringing in the officer so that we see the boy through adult eyes, he makes us recognize that the boys' situation is of great importance to us. Golding then swings the point of view around again, and we are looking with the officer and the boys at the cruiser. In this way Golding forces us to realize that our situation is the same as that of the boys, the officer, and the world in general. What happens to the boys is the same as what is going on in the world war.

STRUCTURE

Structure is the planned framework of the book. It is the deliberate way in which the story is organized by the author to make an impact on the reader.

The novel opens abruptly: We are immediately with the boys on the island, asked to accept their presence there, and swept into a story so engrossing that we just keep turning pages.

The middle of the story is spun out slowly and artfully through the repetitions of mirroring scenes and the steady buildup of tension. In the beginning the boys explored the island and saw it and themselves as glamorous. Later, terrified of the beast, they go looking for it in a scene that recalls the first exploration but reveals their failed dreams and growing disillusionment. This creates tension in the reader.

The boys' repeated use of the chant does the same thing. When they slaughter the first pig, they shout, "Kill the pig!" Later this becomes "Kill the beast!" One chant recalls the other, and the change of a word intensifies the meaning.

Tension is also created by the steady falling away of civilization, which the reader is made aware of early in the story. It begins innocently with the boys' inability to keep rules they've made for themselves because they would rather play. In each chapter there is something which indicates this loss, and the reader begins to anticipate and worry about what will happen next. The author is a master at creating tension.

Once the reader becomes thoroughly absorbed, the story concludes with the same abruptness with which it began. At the end the reader is so caught up by events that he or she has totally suspended disbelief or objectivity and just wants to know what is going to happen to Ralph. The ending's impact is powerful because there is no time for the reader to question or disagree. The story is over and has made its impression before we realize it.

Golding seduces his readers into nonthinking—the very failing he criticizes in the boys. Only after the story has been read, felt, and thought about can the reader understand the danger of being seduced by the automatic acceptance of an idea without due consideration of the facts.

The Story

CHAPTER ONE

The opening chapter introduces us to the characters and the conflict and poses a question: If people were dropped on a distant island that offered plenty of food and no dangerous conditions, would the experience be a good one or a bad one?

Ralph is the first person we meet. He wanders out of the jungle, followed by a fat boy. Although they were dropped by a plane that was under attack during an atomic war, Ralph thinks he is in a paradise. It's especially wonderful because there aren't any adults around.

But is it really? The first paragraph gives you a clue to what the author thinks about the island. There is a "long scar smashed into the jungle" where the plane dropped them the night before. As Ralph breaks through the creepers (even that word says something), a red and yellow bird, the color of fire and heat, flashes into the sky with a "witch-like cry." Ralph stands among the "skull-like coconuts." These are subtle suggestions that the author thinks the island is not quite what the boys expect.

Ralph wears a belt with a snake-clasp that also implies menace. Snakes are an important symbol that we will encounter again.

Ralph doesn't see any of this. It's a wonderful setup for playing, he thinks, and he turns cartwheels. At twelve Ralph is strong, tall, and handsome; a natural athlete, he has been swimming since he was five. He drops his clothes in the same way he willingly leaves the world behind. He has returned to Eden.

A fair-haired boy, Ralph is often described in the presence of sunlight, which implies goodness and naturalness. "A golden light danced and shattered just over his face." He looks at his shadow and thinks it's green. Ralph accepts his new surroundings easily; he's at home on the island.

The fat boy who follows Ralph is worried. An asthmatic, nearly blind without glasses, he sees his life easily threatened because of his weaknesses. He doesn't belong in a wild place like this, and he knows it. He has diarrhea from eating the fruit: The jungle is making him sick.

When he asks Ralph his name, we realize that not all of the boys on the plane knew each other. Ralph is not polite enough to ask his in return, but the fat boy reveals his dreaded nickname, Piggy. When he tries to tell Ralph his real name, he is interrupted by Ralph's teasing, and we never learn Piggy's real name. Ralph is not intentionally mean when he mocks Piggy. He's just not very sensitive or aware, and he's too busy playing to be thoughtful.

NOTE: The Use of Names   Names are significant in *Lord of the Flies*. The main characters' names have something to do with their roles in the story. Certain boys' names we never learn; the littluns and biguns are groups of boys known only by their size. Some boys lose their names, and one forgets his by the end of the story. When you read old legends and tales, you find that characters were cautious about revealing their names. A person was believed to have power over another if he knew his name. A man who wanted to protect himself against his enemies made up a name and did not tell his real one. Keep names, naming, and the loss of a name in mind as you read.

By asking Ralph's name, Piggy shows he is anxious to keep relations civilized and decent while they're on the island. He needs to link himself to civilization and sanity in order to believe he will be safe.

Ralph floats in the warm waters of the lagoon, day-dreaming comfortably. He's too happy with his new-found freedom to worry, and he believes his father will rescue them.

NOTE: Thinking your father will come to save you is like believing in a magical wizard or even a god. According to Golding, this is part of Ralph's innocence and an important idea to be aware of in the story.

Piggy doesn't agree about their chances of being rescued: "We may stay here till we die." His father is dead and therefore won't be rescuing him. Piggy's ability to predict, his near-blindness, and his glasses are characteristics that will have significance in the course of the novel. We will discuss their importance later, but if you follow them through the story, you will increase your understanding of what Golding is saying.

The differences between Ralph and Piggy are obvious. Ralph is strong, handsome, and unthinking; Piggy is fat, serious, and concerned. Together, Ralph and Piggy are like the body and mind of a single person. Ralph enjoys himself sensually while Piggy keeps asking questions, trying to think things through. It is Piggy who knows to blow on the shell to call the boys together; it is Ralph who has the necessary strength to sound the conch shell. And when he does, the boys begin to emerge from the jungle.

NOTE: The Symbolism of the Conch The sounding of the conch is like a reenactment of an ancient event. The boys are being called out of the jungle in much the same way primitive men were called together. At the same time, the conch's sounding is a means of communication, a way of gathering the boys. It brings them out of isolation so they can become a group, a civilization, where they can think together. It calls them away from primitiveness and toward awareness.

In the course of the story, Golding creates events and details that have many interpretations. Perhaps you can see a level of meaning in the story that we have not mentioned. Try to follow it all the way to the conclusion; see if it remains consistent and important.

The twins Sam and Eric are among the first to arrive after the conch is sounded. Piggy can't tell them apart or keep their names straight.

Along the beach comes a band of choirboys dressed in black robes and moving as one creature. The creature is led by Jack Merridew, and the association of Jack with a black creature is an important foreshadowing. We are told that Jack is redheaded and quick to anger. We see Jack make the choirboys stand at attention in the sun until one boy, Simon, faints.

Jack wants to know who is in charge. Ralph introduces himself and invites Jack to join the group. In an attempt to establish order, Piggy tries to learn all the names. Jack mocks Piggy by calling him "Fatty." Ralph quickly defends him but reveals Piggy's nickname, and Jack's ridicule becomes worse. The entire group laughs at Piggy.

This early scene sets up the conflict and reveals the direction the story will take. Ralph knows his basic goodness by defending Piggy and his ineptness by giving away the nickname. Jack's treatment of Piggy calls attention to his dangerous nature and sheds light on his future relationship with Piggy. Piggy is upset that everyone knows and ridicules his name; this makes him vulnerable before the group and especially with Jack.

After all have assembled, the boys elect Ralph as their chief. Golding says that "there was a stillness about Ralph . . . and . . . there was the conch. The being that had blown that, had sat waiting for them. . . ." The boys assume that there is some special quality to Ralph and the conch. They don't even consider Piggy or Jack.

NOTE: The idea that people invest other people and objects with power is important in this story. You will see that Ralph and the conch are given importance and that later that importance is taken away. Some characters, such as Piggy and Simon, who should be regarded as significant, will never be given that respect by the other boys. This is Golding's view of how people allow themselves to believe and disbelieve in people and ideas without considering what is real.

The boys decide to find out whether they are alone on the island. While surveying with Ralph and Simon, Jack says they are true "explorers." The word "glamorous" is used to describe how they feel about themselves and the island. Joyously they heave a boulder over a ledge just to watch it smash on the rocks—an action that foreshadows the falling of other rocks later in the book.

From atop the mountain, Ralph, Jack, and Simon see that the island is "boat-shaped" and feel like men on a ship rushing toward an adventure. This idea of men on a ship moving toward an appointed destiny is repeated at the story's climax, and in it we find hints of the author's profound understanding of human nature.

As the boys descend the mountain, Simon admires the beauty of the candle bushes. Ralph thinks them useless because they don't shed light, and Jack slashes one with his knife. Here again Golding gives us clues of what is to come. The boys encounter a pig, but they are unable to kill it. Although Jack has been talking about hunting for food, he hesitates to stab. "The pause" of the knife "was only long enough for them to understand what an enormity the downward stroke would be."

These are boys playing out their fantasy of life on a deserted island, a life without adult rules. They recognize instinctively that the "cutting into living flesh" and the "unbearable blood" will destroy the game. Yet Jack begins to practice stabbing, and he promises a kill next time.

CHAPTER TWO

At the second assembly, a small boy with a mulberry birthmark talks about the beast in the jungle. After the group has built the first fire with the aid of Piggy's glasses, the boy is found to be missing and thought dead.

Returned from the exploration, Ralph calls an assembly to establish rules. " 'Hands up' like at school," Ralph says. Only the person holding the conch may speak. Thus the conch represents the order they will try to maintain and respect.

Jack says that Ralph is right. "We've got to have rules and obey them. After all, we're not savages. We're English, and the English are best at everything."

For now Ralph and Jack sit side by side on a log and try to convey the beauty of the island to the others. But the little ones (called little 'uns, and later littluns) grow frightened that they may not be rescued. Ralph says, "It's like in a book."

NOTE: The Natural-Goodness-of-Man Theory All the boys have read adventure stories such as *Treasure Island*, *Robinson Crusoe*, and *Swiss Family Robinson*. One idea which these books share is that man is corrupted by living in civilization. If he could be put back into a more natural setting, such as a deserted island or a paradise, he would revert to his original state of goodness. The boys never question this concept of innocence in the books they've read. They believe it, and they want to be like the people they've read about. *Lord of the Flies* is an attempt to disprove this theory of the natural goodness of man.

Throughout the novel the author will let you know his thoughts about the state of man's heart. He will also try to convince you of what he believes. By the end of the story you may agree with him, but you don't have to. You're entitled to your own opinion about whether the forces of good are stronger or weaker than the forces of evil—or whether there are such forces at all. But you will need to be able to support your opinion with evidence from the novel. Notice the events as they are described. Do you believe they would really take place? Would you be more likely to follow Ralph, Piggy, Jack, or Simon? Or would you have an entirely different attitude?

The boys are convinced that they'll have a good time and be like heroes in a book—until a boy with "a mulberry-colored birthmark" on his face speaks. He wants to know what they're going to do about the snakelike beastie he's seen in the woods. At first the others laugh, but as the child persists, they become more and more uneasy. All of them know what it's like to have nightmares or be scared by the dark.

The little boy says it came in the dark, and "in the morning it turned into them things like ropes in the trees and hung in the branches."

NOTE: The beastie, the snakelike thing, is an important symbol. What the boy with a birthmark says hints at the changing nature and beliefs about the beast. The boys' thinking about the beast will change throughout the story. Here they are talking about an actual creature, a snakelike thing that may be present on the island with them.

Ralph doesn't know how to handle the little boy's fear of the beast. He offers logical reasoning: "You only get them in big countries, like Africa, or India." Ralph can't convince them that the beast does not exist. And he doesn't have the intelligence to consider the existence of a beast in some abstract form. Frustrated, Ralph can only suggest that they build a fire to assure their rescue.

Jack appears to agree with Ralph, then adds, "But if there was a snake we'd hunt it and kill it." With that statement, Jack allows for the beast's possible existence, and this terrifies the boys. It is important to follow Jack's use of terror in the course of events.

In the second scene the boys assemble logs and leaves atop the mountain, only to realize they have no means of starting a fire. Jack snatches Piggy's glasses from his face, leaving him howling with fear, for Piggy is almost blind without his glasses. Recall that Piggy is the book's representative of civilization; when he loses his glasses, the link to a rational world is momentarily severed.

NOTE: Sight, Blindness, Fire, and the Mountain
Being able to see and being blind have always been important themes in literature. In Piggy's case, his glasses imply that he sees or knows more than most of the other boys. He is more concerned with maintaining a civilized and orderly life on the island. He "sees" what will happen if they aren't able to do this.

The glasses symbolize the link to civilization, but at the same time they show Piggy's impaired ability. While Piggy knows or sees than Ralph, he does not see the total situation on the island. In addition to his real visual problems, Piggy's vision of what the jungle represents is impaired. He will come to blame his and the boys' troubles on Jack, and he will never fully recognize the true situation. Thus Piggy can have the ability to see or understand more than most people and at the same time not be able to see his immediate situation clearly. Often in literature the inability of a character to see clearly around himself enables him to see the future. This usually marks him as a fool to the people around him and subjects him to the ridicule of those less perceptive than he.

Fire on a mountain is a complex symbol in literature. The mountain represents a place where man has
gone to pray; fire represents humanity's hope. By
lighting a fire on the mountain, primitive man was
telling his gods: We're scared to be alone. You must be
out there; tell us what to do. This is what the boys are
saying, symbolically, when they light the fire.

The boys cheer as the fire grows. "The flames, as
though they were a kind of wild life, crept as a jaguar
creeps on its belly toward a line of birch-like saplings."
The fire is described as a wild beast. The boys fall
"silent, feeling the beginnings of awe at the power set
free."

Piggy peers "nervously into hell" and says, "him
with the mark on his face. . . . Him that talked about
the snakes. He was down there—"

"Tall swathes of creepers rose for a moment into
view, agonized, and went down again." The little
boys scream, "Snakes! Snakes!" The boy with the
mulberry birthmark has apparently been killed by the
fire; the beast he feared in the creepers has taken
him.

The concept of feared things becoming the enemy is
one you'll want to keep in mind. It has a great deal to
do with the ultimate meaning of the story.

What began as paradise has somehow turned into
hell. Something is wrong. There are snakes in paradise, and Ralph's having a snake-clasp on his belt suggests that the boys have brought the snakes with
them. This wasn't in any of the adventure books the
boys read. Golding is giving us fair warning that the
theory of man's natural goodness may have serious
flaws.

CHAPTER THREE

Jack practices stalking a pig and Ralph tries to build shelters; Simon goes off into the jungle to meditate.

Jack is alone in the jungle. Notice the description of his surroundings: "The silence of the forest was more oppressive than the heat, and at this hour of the day there was not even the whine of insects. Only when Jack himself roused a gaudy bird from a primitive nest of sticks was the silence shattered and echoes set ringing by a harsh cry that seemed to come out of the abyss of ages." The jungle is threatening; it is a metaphor for what is dark, dangerous, and wild in someone's mind. Jack is learning to be comfortable where most of us would be lost.

In the same passage, Jack is said to be "dog-like, uncomfortably on all fours yet unheeding his discomfort." He closes his eyes and raises his head, breathing in "gently with flared nostrils, assessing the current of warm air for information."

Golding's description of Jack is filled with animal references. Jack is acquiring the dangerous and threatening ways of the jungle. He is learning to hunt like an animal by depending on his senses of smell, sight, sound, and movement. Sniffing the warm, steamy pig droppings, Jack becomes more primitive and dismisses his human inclinations. His chase after the pigs is described as "the promise of meat." Jack misses his prey again, but this only serves to fuel his determination to kill.

NOTE: Many references to Jack and Ralph make use of dark and light imagery. Jack is described as being comfortable in the dark jungle, and he can even see in the dark, much like an animal. Ralph is building shelters to protect the boys from darkness and the unknown beast of the jungle; he is a champion of light.

When Jack returns to the lagoon where Ralph and Simon are finding it difficult to build shelters, he has trouble explaining his desire to kill. Jack is slowly becoming an animal and is unable to express his longings. He is so caught up in learning to hunt that he can't remember why they should be rescued. Ralph, on the other hand, is trying to learn to express his thoughts; he is groping toward an understanding of what it means to be a person. "He wanted to explain how people were never quite what you thought they were."

To avoid an argument, Ralph and Jack discuss the fear of the beast, which is getting worse among the smallest boys. Simon says: "As if . . . the beastie or the snake-thing, was real." Jack and Ralph both shudder.

The fear of the beast in the jungle is so great that no one mentions it by name anymore. Remember the idea of naming? If the boys can't give a name to what they fear, it has gained power over them.

Jack makes fun by calling them all batty, which diminishes the tension. Yet moments later he says, "There's nothing in it of course. Just a feeling. But you can feel as if you're not hunting, but—being hunted, as if something's behind you all the time in the jungle."

Jack denies the existence of an actual beast by ridiculing those who believe in it. However, he recognizes the presence of "something" lurking in the jungle that Ralph is unable to accept. Jack knows what the littluns feel, but rather than fearing it, Jack is attracted to the presence in the jungle.

The conflict between the two main characters is mounting. Ralph believes the only solution is to keep the fire going in order to assure their rescue. Because the well-tended fire is also a form of light, it may be considered a symbol of knowledge and/or communication. You might say Ralph stands for the positive forces and Jack represents the darker, negative, and lesser known urges of mankind. Ralph and Jack are described as "two continents of experience and feeling, unable to communicate." Because neither is able to listen to the other and their differences in opinion are growing stronger, a clash must eventually take place.

The closing scene of the chapter is Simon's. Much like Jack, he goes alone and unafraid into the jungle. But compare Simon's jungle with Jack's. The harshness is portrayed, but so is the beauty: "With the fading of the light the riotous colors died and the heat and urgency cooled away. The candlebuds stirred. Their green sepals drew back a little and the white tips of the flowers rose delicately." Simon loves nature, and the description here is filled with a sense of awe for it. Simon is like a mystic who goes into the wilderness to pray, and the jungle shows him its undetected beauty. Butterflies often follow him.

Like Jack and Ralph, Simon knows there is no real beast in the jungle. However, Simon is not afraid to call the fear of the beast by name. And there is power in being able to call something by its true name.

Simon is kinder and more compassionate than the other boys. Simon (his name originally meant one who hears) hears and understands more than most people his age, and he has the quiet courage to attempt an explanation of what he knows. But his task is impossible because no one on the island can appreciate what he says. Ralph and Jack label him an odd-ball because they can't understand him.

CHAPTER FOUR

A ship passes the island while Jack is leading the hunters, their faces painted, on an expedition to kill a pig. Jack breaks one lens of Piggy's glasses.

A lengthy and important narrative at the beginning of the chapter gives us the impression that months have passed. The boys no longer clock the hours of day and night. The civilization they've known is dropping away; like primitive man, they are being guided by the sun and stars.

This section describes the different times of day as though they were different times of life. Morning is seen as childhood, "a time when play was good and life so full that hope was not necessary and therefore forgotten."

The middle of the day is likened to the difficulties of middle life. "Strange things happened at midday. . . . Sometimes land loomed where there was no land and flicked out like a bubble as the children watched." Exhausted by the heat, the boys dismiss the mirages they see without trying to understand them. The inability to understand what might be happening around them and the necessary acceptance of living without explanations are equated with the middle years of a person's life—a time when there are often denial, ignorance, and confusion.

Late in the day the boys are more comfortable, but they begin to dread the onset of evening. Similarly, late in life a person may experience freedom from confusion, but by then the closeness of death looms large.

Golding says that late afternoon is a "time of comparative coolness but menaced by the coming of the dark." Night, or being near death, fills one with "restlessness, under the remote stars." When a person is near death, all that is associated with the living universe becomes distant.

NOTE: Golding's Metaphor for Life   Why does the author include this commentary in a tale about a bunch of boys trying to survive on an island? Golding is offering us his philosophy that life starts out playfully and ends anxiously. The passage holds the key to some of the story's deeper meaning. We all begin as playful children, move slowly and painfully into adulthood, and anxiously approach death. This is a story about young boys coming of age or approaching the end of innocence. We see them young and playful at the beginning, and we will find them elderly in spirit by the end. The activity of boys on an island is also a metaphor for the human race's struggle to survive. The earth is our island, and some people are trying to build shelters while others are hunting pigs. Only a few see messages in the mirage; most are blinded.

Piggy, who has impaired vision, dismisses along with the others the "mysteries" and the "miraculous" on the island. It is he who labels the strange happenings a mirage. Although no mention is made here of Simon, he is the one who does not dismiss the wonder and the terror of mirages, as we will see later.

NOTE: Mirage as Metaphor   An important idea underlies Golding's use of mirages. A mirage is something that does not really exist yet has a power of suggestion that can impress a person and influence how he acts and thinks. For example, if you were thirsty and thought you saw water, but the water was only a mirage, you would probably feel even more thirsty because of the very idea of water. The glands in your throat which cause you to feel thirst will react just as strongly to real water as to imagined water.

Here mirage introduces the idea of the suggestive power of something which does not really exist. In daylight the boys ignore mirages seen in nature, such as the palm trees which seem to float in the sky, but mirages of the night, like the beast in the jungle, cannot be so easily dismissed.

Invisible things also influence how people act and think. We watch Roger throwing stones at a littlun called Henry. He doesn't hit Henry; "there was a space round Henry . . . into which he dare not throw. Here, invisible yet strong, was the taboo of the old life. Round the squatting child was the protection of parents and school and policemen and the law." Something invisible, like a concept, the concept of civilization, has the power to control human thought and actions. We can think of civilization as an invisible mirage. It does really exist, and it has power over us if we hold the concept in our head. When we do, it influences our behavior and thought, as it keeps Roger from hitting Henry. When we stop believing in the concept of civilized ways, the concept ceases to have power over us.

For Roger and the other boys, civilization is a mirage that is slipping away. Their hair is growing long and wild, their nails are becoming claws, and they are "filthy dirty." They are also beginning to do things that would not be acceptable at home.

Jack calls Roger into the jungle to paint their faces with clay and charcoal. Their masks will camouflage them; they will be a part of the jungle when hunting pig. With his own face painted, Jack "looked in astonishment, no longer at himself but at an awesome stranger." He is ceasing to be himself, and the mask is becoming "a thing on its own, behind which Jack hid, liberated from shame and self-consciousness." Jack dances and his laughter becomes "a bloodthirsty snarling." Jack is losing his human identity and his self-awareness. He can even act like an animal in front of the others; he no longer cares what they think. And the others feel "compelled" to follow the creature with the masked face. Jack goes off with his hunters to track pig.

In the second scene, Ralph spots a passing ship on the horizon. "Balanced on a high peak of need, agonized by indecision, Ralph cried out: 'Oh God, oh God!' " Till now Ralph has childishly believed— needed to believe—that they would be rescued, that someone would come along and save them. This vague notion has allowed him to play away his time as though he were just one of the little boys. Jack and the hunters have betrayed Ralph by abandoning what is most important to him, the fire. Ralph realizes he will have to take action.

From around the "unfriendly side of the mountain," where the beast supposedly lives, come the chanting choirboys led by Jack. The twins, who are part of the procession, are described as "errant"—a word that foreshadows the twins' eventual betrayal of Ralph. And what Simon sees, looking from Ralph to

Jack, "seemed to make him afraid." The final, irreversible split has taken place between Jack and Ralph. Simon understands that the two can no longer be friends. This is the first in a series of mounting crises between Jack and Ralph.

Jack is triumphant as he leads his frenzied mob back with a slaughtered pig. He cannot contain his joy at the power he felt "when they closed in on the struggling pig, knowledge that they had outwitted a living thing, imposed their will upon it, taken away its life like a long satisfying drink." Jack and the boys have found a way of not feeling their fears; killing another living creature helps them to forget the beast in the jungle.

Enraged by betrayal and dashed hope, Ralph thrusts himself into the role of leader. "There was a ship," he says, making it clear that hunting is less important to the chief than fire. When the hunters begin to understand "the dismal truth" about going home, their sentiments betray Jack's sense of the importance of the kill.

"The two boys faced each other. There was the brilliant world of hunting, tactics, fierce exhilaration, skill; and there was the world of longing and baffled common-sense." For Ralph and Jack this is the beginning of all-out war. The battle will be between the thrill of power and force and the difficult and disillusioning struggle to maintain hope and good sense. Ralph and Jack will struggle without either of them fully understanding the forces at work in him.

Ralph's stance is much more passive, a waiting that must be done and a very uncertain waiting. Who is it that will come for them? Rescuers or the beast? There's no wait on Jack's side, only the illusory but exhilarating feel of gaining power over the fear which haunts them.

That Jack breaks Piggy's glasses out of spite is inevitable. Piggy's link to civilization is partly destroyed, making his situation with Jack and the jungle even more dangerous. Simon returns the broken glasses, and "passions beat about Simon on the mountain-top with awful wings." With their hopes dashed, violence and blood lust simmering, and civilization receding, Simon knows they are endangered.

Power plays between Ralph and Jack fill the rest of the scene. Jack apologizes for breaking the glasses and gains the hunters' admiration. Ralph, no longer fooled by Jack's empty words, insists that he rebuild the fire immediately. But then Ralph refuses to move out of the way, which forces Jack to build the fire in a different place.

For the first time Ralph recognizes Piggy's importance. "Not even Ralph knew how a link between him and Jack had been snapped and fastened elsewhere. 'I'll bring 'em back,' " he says to Piggy as he borrows his glasses to light the fire.

New allegiances have been made. The friendship between Ralph and Jack is broken; their relationship is now that of enemies. And Ralph has bonded himself in friendship to Piggy.

More power struggles! Ralph tries not to eat roast pig and Jack tries not to give him any "as an assertion of power." Piggy the powerless leaves himself open to further ridicule from Jack when he asks for food. It's Simon who shows compassion by sharing his food.

"Inexpressible frustrations combined to make his rage elemental and awe-inspiring," and Jack begins a chantlike recitation of the kill: "I painted my face—I stole up. Now you eat—all of you—and I—" Jack's words are becoming more primitive all the time. He is an early hunter learning to grunt out the first words that represent thought. But instead of enlarging his thinking, Jack is slipping backward.

As Jack tells the story of the killing, a brutal joy infects the group. The boys join in making primitive sounds, "pig-dying noises." Jack is calling them backward into mindlessness. A reenactment begins with Maurice playing pig. They are little boys playing at a good game; at the same time, they are dangerously close to being savages. Ralph, who is part boy, part man, watches "envious and resentful." The leader side of him won't allow his little boy side to play; it makes him angry that he has to act like a man.

"I'm calling an assembly. With the conch." With his belief in the conch, symbol of communication and awareness, Ralph has no choice but to call the boys away from Jack and toward self-consciousness.

CHAPTER FIVE

Ralph calls a meeting to talk about what's important for the boys' survival. Jack breaks up the assembly with a frenzied dance.

NOTE: The Use of Irony   Golding's use of irony becomes more obvious as the story continues. You can recognize irony when something is said to be true and you know that the exact opposite is in fact true. For example, Jack says that the boys are not "savages," but that's exactly what they turn out to be. And not only can *we* spot the irony in the events and conversations of the story, but Ralph, the character in the story, is also aware of irony. This shared perception allows us to be close to Ralph and to experience the situation along with him, yet the irony forces us to step back and think about what the author is saying.

Bringing us close to the action while keeping us distant from it is a deliberate device that Golding uses repeatedly. It will force us to think about our own attitudes, and it will give us a picture of the world beyond ourselves.

The irony of Ralph's situation begins to present itself to him. As he walks along the beach, trying to think, he can't help "remembering that first enthusiastic exploration as though it were part of a brighter childhood." Once he had daydreamed and pretended, like the characters he'd read about in books; now he considers how wearisome life really is. He has to figure out everything for himself: "every path was an improvisation." Suddenly he realizes that a big part of life is just keeping alive and out of danger: "a considerable part of one's waking life was spent watching one's feet." Ralph smiles "jeeringly." He sees the gap between what he hoped life on the island would be and what that life is turning out to be. He also recognizes that the Ralph he used to be and the Ralph he's becoming are opposites.

And he doesn't like "perpetually flicking the tangled hair out of his eyes." Ralph wants civilization back; he doesn't want to be dirty and wild. He is slowly moving toward an adult awareness of his needs.

Ralph tries to think about leadership of the boys. Being chief is beginning to mean he has to act like a chief! ("You had to think, you had to be wise.") Again there is irony. Recall how playfully Ralph took on the role; it was all a game then, but now he thinks that "the meeting must not be fun, but business." Ralph is growing up, and he has to "adjust his values." What he thought once is no longer true; he is being forced to change.

Ralph's growing up creates in him a dawning awareness of others. He appreciates Piggy's friendship more and respects his ability to think. Ralph talks to the assemblies in such a way that everyone, even the littlest boys, will understand what he has to say. He wants to establish in everyone's mind—but also in his own—what is important. He calls it "what's what," meaning what's really important.

For the first time Ralph recognizes the seriousness of the situation and acts responsibly. And Ralph wants the others to understand and adjust their values also. He takes an adult stand.

"We've got to make smoke up there—or die." Ralph tells the group what he expects of them so that they may remain civilized and be rescued or survive. Ironically, the smoke that the others try to kill him with at the end of the book is what saves them all.

"Things are breaking up. I don't understand why." For all his growing authority, Ralph cannot understand what's happening to them. Recall the idea of confusion when a person reaches midlife; Ralph falls into confusion as he tries to understand adult problems. Even when he links "the beastie, the snake, the fire, the talk of fear," he doesn't recognize that all these fears are one fear, the fear of the unknown, symbolized by the jungle beast.

If Ralph had been a truly wise leader, he might have ended the meeting at this point, but he chooses to go on. With darkness beginning to surround them, they attempt a rational discussion about the fear. Can anyone talk about ghosts in the middle of a dark forest, or even in a dark house, without scaring himself? It's impossible; yet Ralph tries!

Jack is the only one who can talk about the fear, and

what he says is true: "Fear can't hurt you any more than a dream. There aren't any beasts to be afraid of on this island." But, as Jack always does, he denies the beast and then turns around and implies his ability to kill it if it does exist. "Am I a hunter or am I not?" This is Jack's "what's what," hunting and killing.

Piggy also gets to say his "what's what." As reasonable proof that a beast can't exist on the island, he asks, "What would a beast eat?" The littluns make a game of it: "Pig," they say. "We eat pig," Piggy says, and the littluns shout, "Piggy!" There is irony in the use of the name Piggy and the fact that the boys kill and eat pig: It hints that Piggy will be killed by a beast, but not the one they fear. In a subtle way that nobody understands, not even Piggy, he is saying that they are the beast because they kill and eat pig.

Piggy tries to consider the problem as a grownup would. Life is scientific, he says, believing that everything can be explained. Then notice how his poor use of English undermines what he says and tells the real truth: "there isn't no beast" and "there isn't no fear, either." He means that the beast does not exist, but because two negatives make a positive, he is actually saying that it does exist.

He also tries to explain away fear by bringing forward the littluns who are scared. Of course this backfires when little Phil says he's seen something walking around at night. Then Percival comes forward, reciting his name and address the way many young children are taught to do in case they get lost. When he can't recall his telephone number, Percival is desolated and can only cry. The other littluns cry too as they all "share in a sorrow that was universal." All the littluns are lost, and the biguns are losing their childhoods. The boys and their loss reflect a world that has lost its way.

Percival also introduces a new understanding of the beast. The beast comes out of the sea, he says. The boys panic! The beast could be anywhere! It is not just a snake or some pig-eating creature from the unfriendly side of the mountain; the beast could be anything! This opens the way for many things to be called the beast. Hysteria reigns.

Simon tries to explain what he knows. "Maybe there is a beast. . . . Maybe it's only us." But Jack's cruel mockery of that idea and the boys' terror defeat Simon. He becomes "inarticulate in his effort to express mankind's essential illness." He already surmises the truth, that evil resides within man's nature. Simon is the only one who could save them, but Jack destroys that chance.

NOTE: Golding's Views on Civilization   Here again is another strong hint of what the author is telling us about mankind in his metaphor of boys stranded on an island. Mankind, Golding says, would like to believe that civilization is evil and that nature is pure. That's why we have *Tarzan of the Apes* and *Swiss Family Robinson*. But Golding believes something different, that we need civilization and its schools, policemen, and laws in order to keep us from throwing stones at each other. Without such things we would all be savages. Stripped of civilization, the beast surfaces.

According to Golding, the beast resides within us, and that is what Simon understands and tries to explain. However, his attempt only serves to heighten everyone's terror because they can't understand what he is really saying. They can't hear the meaning behind the words. Even Piggy does not understand.

The meeting continues to break down and to slip away from Ralph's control. His original good intentions have had disastrous results. In effect the author is saying that evil often comes out of good. Too late Ralph realizes that "we ought to have left all this for daylight." He and they are defenseless against the mirages of the night. On the mountain he was sure that he had to call a meeting, but he's been undermined by his own decisions.

A vote is taken on the question of whether or not ghosts exist, and we are reminded of the first time the boys voted. This poll is filled with terror and darkness. Again the irony makes a point about how things ought to be and how they really are.

After the vote Piggy asks, "What are we? Humans? Or animals? Or savages?" These are the questions the book attempts to answer.

Jack wants to know why they should listen to Ralph, whom they chose as chief. "Why should choosing make any difference?" The question is an important one. Jack, who believes in the use of force and fear, sees no point in choice. But choice is what distinguishes human beings from animals who operate on instinct and savages who do no thinking. Choice is the answer to Piggy's question; we are human only if we have choice.

Ralph shouts at Jack, "You're breaking the rules!" Jack responds, "Who cares?" And Ralph answers, "Because the rules are the only thing we've got." The rules that we as human beings choose to make are the only thing that keeps us from being animals.

But Jack cannot be made to understand. "We're strong—we hunt!" Again he uses primitive language. "If there's a beast, we'll hunt it down! We'll close in and beat and beat and beat—!" Jack will kill the beast in the jungle by freeing the beast within himself. He leads the others into a mock hunt.

"Blow the conch," Piggy whispers, but Ralph has lost the assurance of his leadership. Now he is uncertain of his power over Jack and the others. His first good decision to be responsible has met failure, and he's not ready to face a second mistake.

"If you don't blow," Piggy says, "we'll soon be animals." Piggy too recognizes the degeneration that is taking place.

Still Ralph hesitates. "Are there ghosts? Or beasts?" Ralph can't figure out what he still doesn't understand. The beliefs he held in the past are crumbling, and he doesn't know what to trust.

"Course there aren't," Piggy says, holding to his rational vision of the world. " 'Cos things wouldn't make sense. Houses an' streets, an'—TV." Piggy still wants to believe that everything can be explained, that life is scientific.

"But s'pose they don't make sense?" Ralph asks, forced to consider ideas that civilization has always protected him from or that he has been too young to think about. What if things don't make sense? Then what? What is there? What matters in life? These are hard questions to answer. Ralph shudders, for if life doesn't make sense or has no organized meaning, then no one may ever come for them. And if that's true, maybe there is a beast who is "watching and waiting" for them.

Piggy can't take this kind of talk because it means his adult world is not as safe as he wants to believe. It means his fat asthmatic body doesn't stand a chance.

"Three blind mice," Ralph says of himself, Piggy, and Simon. They are no match for Jack. Ralph wants to give up, but Simon and Piggy want him to go on being chief, for they recognize that Ralph is their only chance. But everything seems pointless to Ralph, even keeping the fire going. He has begun to surrender his faith and hope.

Piggy says that grownups "ain't afraid of the dark. They'd meet and have tea and discuss." The irony here may be the cruelest in the story: The boys are on the island only because adults *can't* sit and discuss. Adults are as much afraid of the dark as the boys.

"If only they could get a message to us." Ralph says, "a sign or something." But Ralph's prayer has a desperate and disillusioned tone. As the chapter closes, Ralph is filled with fears of failure and doom and does not blow the conch. Piggy has said that if he doesn't blow it, they will soon be animals, and Piggy's vision of the future is accurate.

As if to comment on the mood of hopelessness and despair, Percival cries out from a bad dream. He is "living through circumstances in which the incantation of his address was powerless to help him." Percy's memorization of his address is of no avail in the jungle; the nightmare that terrifies him terrifies all of them, awake or asleep.

We can think about Ralph at this point as if he were two different people: The Ralph at the beginning of the book is very different from the Ralph at the end of this chapter. And Golding's use of irony suggests that we need to be part of civilization and away from nature in order to exist.

CHAPTER SIX

The twins see the beast at dawn and wake Ralph. The boys go looking for it on the far side of the island.

As if in answer to Ralph's prayers for a signal from the adult world, something falls from the heavens and lands on the mountain. A dead man, "a figure . . . with dangling limbs," floats down in a parachute, a casualty of the battle overhead. More irony! The answer to Ralph's prayer is powerless to help them; the adult world can do little for the boys. There is even greater irony here in that the boys will convince themselves that the dead man who moves like a puppet is the beast. Thus the hoped-for rescuers and the beast have much in common.

The beast who terrifies their dreams and makes them fear the jungle is nothing but a man caught up in strings. If the twins, who were supposed to be tending the fire, had stayed awake, they would have seen him floating down and might have saved the boys from ignorance. But Sam and Eric "could never manage to do things sensibly if that meant acting independently." Sam could hardly have stayed awake to watch the sky and the jungle while Eric slept.

The description of the fire they rebuild reminds us of the boys' first menacing fire. Eric, watching "the scurrying woodlice that were so frantically unable to avoid the flames," doesn't want to think about that first fire. Again and again Golding uses one event to remind us of a previous event and to hint of a coming one. In this way the details of the novel seem to mirror one another and intensify our reactions to the story.

"Wasn't he waxy?" Sam and Eric recall how upset Ralph was that the fire died when the hunters followed Jack. They equate Ralph with a teacher they had at school, seeing Ralph now as an adult, someone not to be friends with but to be avoided. Samneric's attitude indicates how the younger boys feel toward Ralph: He is acting too much like an adult. Samneric are glad that Ralph "went for" Jack and that they escaped the blame for having abandoned the fire.

Childishly, they are enjoying their good luck—and then they see "the beast" on the mountain.

Ralph is dreaming of home when the twins wake him. In the early morning light he holds up the conch to signal the boys. Whether it is fear of his shaky rule over them or fear of the beast's hearing, he does not blow. Only the sunlight, a "growing slice of gold," reduces their fears enough that they can talk about what to do.

"This'll be a real hunt!" Jack's remark tells us he's thrilled.

Ralph believes the twins are telling the truth, even though much of what they say is exaggeration and hysteria. They turn themselves into heroes and cover up their having let the fire go out again. Ralph doesn't really interrogate them.

The decision is made to search the island, leaving Piggy once again with the littluns. Ralph is more considerate toward Piggy than he was the first time he left him behind. Jack is jealous and verbally assaults Piggy: "This is a hunter's job."

You may see parallels between Ralph and Jack's disagreement about who should take charge of dealing with the beast and our world situation today. Consider the arguments over the nuclear arms race. Some believe we should try to reason with countries who appear to be dangerous; these people are the Ralphs and Piggys of the world, the people who cannot believe there is really a beast that must be warred on. Others feel we must build up arms in order to be ready for the possibility of an attack; they are the Jacks of the world.

In order to deal with Jack's hunger for hunting the beast, Ralph turns the talk away from the beast. He convinces the boys that the fire must be kept going.

The second exploration of the island recalls the first, but the two are very different. Ralph and Simon and Jack were jubilant that first day; now Ralph is brooding and cautious as he picks the direction, Jack leads "with theatrical caution," and Simon ponders his inability to speak before the group.

When they reach the place of the beast, Ralph realizes he has to be the one "to go forward" and face the unknown. This is the right and responsibility of a leader, and Ralph knows he must expose himself. "There was nowhere to hide, even if one did not have to go on." And he discovers what he believed all along: there is no beast.

Jack, acting as though he's concerned about Ralph, comes up behind him. He thinks the spot would make a great fort because of its height. His enthusiasm for hurling rocks over the edge recalls the earlier exploration and promises that other rocks will be hurled over a cliff.

Ralph wants to return to the mountain to start up the fire. "The beast won't be there," Jack says. But that's exactly where it is.

The other boys who have come along decide they want to play on this part of the island, and an argument brews. Ralph wants to return to tend the fire; Jack and the boys want to play in the fort. The tension builds between Jack and Ralph. "I am chief," Ralph says, insistent upon returning.

Like Samneric, the boys have little regard for Ralph's concerns and only want to play. They are annoyed; Ralph is acting too much like an adult or a leader. The last sentence of the chapter begins, "Jack led the way"; more and more the boys are siding with Jack. Ralph is losing his command.

CHAPTER SEVEN

Ralph allows himself to be one of Jack's followers. He is struggling with his role as leader, trying to hang on to it, wanting to let go when Simon makes his prophecy. Ralph gives in to the lust for blood and later sees the beast.

Golding brings us close to Ralph, as though we were thinking his thoughts, stumbling along behind Jack, feeling the forest. He distracts himself with thoughts of cleaning himself, "his toilet." Ralph has made a complete circle in his thinking: Civilization is now the dream, not freedom from it.

All the boys are dirty, not from playing but because they're cut off from the civilizing effects of the world. Their clothing is mostly gone, only tattered pieces remaining to remind them of the past, and filth has become an accepted part of their life. Ralph realizes that he is giving in to the jungle. "He discovered with a little fall of the heart that these were the conditions he took as normal now and that he did not mind."

Ralph's values have adjusted themselves once again. Ralph is discovering he can no longer stand to be isolated from the civilized world and also be set apart from his group. As a human being, he needs the comfort and friendship of the other boys. Without the world he has always known to sustain him, he cannot bear being cut off from his peers. He cannot sustain himself.

Loneliness and the fear of isolation are common human experiences. How often do you do something with your friends, something you would never consider doing alone, just to be with them? These are natural feelings for people of all ages.

The side of the island the boys are exploring differs from the area where the lagoon and the shelters are. "The filmy enchantments of mirage could not endure the cold ocean water and the horizon was hard, clipped blue." The area where the boys live is equated with home and safety—what they long for—but on this side of the island Ralph can't hang on to his illusions of leadership. It's too hard and too lonely, and he feels "numbed" by the indifference of nature to human beings. The sea with its rising and falling tides is vast; if it happens to destroy man in its wake, the sea does not care. It is a moving, living force that has no feelings, does not mind whether Ralph or anyone else lives or dies. "Faced by the brute obtuseness of the ocean, the miles of division, one was clamped down, one was helpless, one was condemned."

Into Ralph's moment of despair Simon whispers like a spirit, "You'll get back to where you came from." Ralph still has the ocean in mind ("It's so big"), but he is struggling with his own smallness, his limited ability to act as leader.

The irony in what Simon appears to be saying prompts Ralph to respond in kind: "Got a ship in your pocket?" Because he has come so far from the person he used to be, Ralph can't fathom getting home again. He's too overwhelmed by the indifference of the world about him, too lost—in a spiritual sense—to find his way back. Simon's statement is prophetic, and his spiritual nature encourages us to believe what he says.

NOTE: The Use of Fable   Some critics argue that *Lord of the Flies* is a fable; others deny this strongly. A fable is a tale in which the characters represent ideas and the events point toward a moral. In a fable we don't usually care much about the characters because they are representations rather than real people. Aesop's "The Tortoise and the Hare" tells us something about competition; we don't worry how the hare felt after losing the race. But we do care about the characters in *Lord of the Flies*, for they are believable people. In that sense, then, the book is not a fable.

However, each of the boys comes to represent something more than just himself. Some readers interpret the story from a political point of view: Ralph represents democratic power, Jack is totalitarian power, and Simon is religion. Another critic may find that the characters stand for psychological concepts. Still others may see the tale in terms of religion, as a battle between good and evil. You may agree or disagree with any of these theories, and you may well discover an entirely different way to understand *Lord of the Flies*.

The important thing is that you notice your own reactions as you read. The boys on the island seem to be reflections of other things we know about. Their plight is ours, and what happens to them will somehow affect us; they offer us insights and ideas about ourselves. If you find this to be true, you may begin to see the events of the story taking on a significance beyond the story itself. In this way *Lord of the Flies* is like a fable, because of the meaning the characters and events take on.

Jack bends down to smell the warm pig droppings "as though he loved them." He does love them! They are an indication that the pig is near and something is about to happen.

Ralph lets Jack take charge of the situation and daydreams about his room at home. When the boar rushes them, Ralph's reflexes are faster than his mind;

he hits the pig, and the thrill of the hunt overtakes him.

There follows an important exchange between Ralph and Jack. Ralph says, "I walloped him properly. That was the beast, I think." Like everyone else who has tried to hunt, Ralph lets his enthusiasm lend to exaggeration. By calling the boar the beast, he creates a link between the two. For now, Jack recognizes that the beast is not a boar and denies it. He doesn't want Ralph to own the glory of having killed the beast.

Ralph and Robert begin a reenactment of hitting the boar, and all the boys join in. This dance is more savage than earlier ones. Robert plays the pig, and he is hit in the rear with sticks. The game quickly gets out of hand amid shouts of "Kill him! Kill him!" Ralph, too, wants "a handful of that brown, vulnerable flesh. The desire to squeeze and hurt was overmastering."

Without the structure and the rules of civilization, the desire to kill surfaces even in Ralph. It cannot be resisted. This is Golding's view of the true nature of man. Civilization is not the corrupter; man carries the problem within him wherever he goes.

Jack says it was a good game, but Ralph's conscience, which he lost touch with when the desire to kill surfaced, now makes him "uneasy." Ralph may be just as vulnerable as the others to the lust for blood, but he is civilized. Whatever impression civilization has made on him, he carries it with him; his awareness of right and wrong can't be permanently erased. He begins to lead again.

The search for the beast resumes, but it's gotten late and Ralph is concerned about Piggy. Again Jack's jealousy is evident, and you want to shout at Ralph, "Pay attention to Jack's feelings!" Ralph doesn't, and you know something will come of this. Jack always retaliates. Simon, treating Ralph as the chief, says he will return to Piggy and the boys.

The tension between Ralph and Jack hangs in the air. Jack wants to be in charge of everything, but Ralph resumes his role as leader. He begins to think again.

Because of Ralph's understanding of himself, his awareness of others, and what he has learned from Piggy, he tries not to compete with Jack. His question to Jack sounds like something Piggy would say: "Why do you hate me?" Ralph knows that Jack wants to be leader, and his question opens up the issue between them. The other boys, sensing the naked sincerity, are embarrassed by what has been asked. "The boys stirred uneasily, as though something indecent had been said."

You could look at it this way: By asking the question openly, Ralph has made himself vulnerable to Jack's scorn. Imagine yourself asking someone that question. To face someone and ask why he or she dislikes you gives that person the opportunity to hurt you. Thus Ralph's attempt is a brave one, a real indication of his courage. It's also foolish, given Jack's personality. Jack is out to hurt because he is jealous. So Ralph is embarrassed and hurt by his own sincerity.

Ralph takes over again, resuming his role as leader, with Jack "brooding" in the rear. No one wants to climb the dark mountain, and Jack uses their fear to goad Ralph about his bravery. "I'm going up the mountain," Jack says, inferring that Ralph is afraid. The anger between them is described as the "fresh rub of two spirits in the dark." There is no way these two can talk to one another; they can only compete.

The two enemies start up the mountain, joined by Roger, who is very much one of Jack's boys. Their journey is like a negative repeat of that joyful first exploration of the island by Ralph, Jack, and Simon. They go in darkness, out of dread and full of hate for each other.

Ralph tries to tell Jack they are foolish in looking for the beast after dark. Perhaps he remembers the terror of the night before. Jack, being Jack, uses the idea of his being afraid against Ralph. And Ralph, unable not to compete with Jack, responds in kind by calling Jack's bluff and sending him on ahead.

Jack goes looking for the beast as Ralph did earlier in the day (Chapter 6). Unlike Ralph, Jack returns terrified at having seen the beast.

Still unable to believe in the existence of a real beast, Ralph challenges within himself the idea. "He bound himself together with his will, fused his fear and loathing into a hatred, and stood up." Terrified, he makes himself look. The moon and the night and the dead parachutist on the mountain create the beast. Although he knows better than to attempt such things after dark, Ralph does it. And Ralph succumbs to fear, for he sees the beast.

CHAPTER EIGHT

Jack challenges Ralph's leadership, then leaves. Later he offers a pig's head to the beast and Simon talks with the Lord of the Flies.

Once the fear of the beast's existence gets into Ralph, the power of the civilized world slips further from his grasp. The shell that has symbolized order is now called a "blob"; the conch is becoming insignificant in the way that civilization is. This symbol is the first of many symbols whose importance to the boys will be diminished.

The boys talk about the reality of the beast. They can't light a signal fire because the beast may see it.

And if they can't do that, Ralph says, "We're beaten." Fire, another symbol, is losing its power to give hope.

Jack is insulted by Ralph's unwillingness to believe that he and the hunters can go after the beast. Jack "inexpertly" blows the conch to call an assembly, thereby bringing to a head the festering problem between him and Ralph. His blowing the conch indicates his desire to take control; that he does it poorly is a comment on his abilities. Jack denounces Ralph's leadership. He accuses Ralph of being like Piggy, that is, being too weak to lead. (Recall Ralph's asking Jack why he hated him, which was something Piggy would do. Jack is correct in saying that Ralph is acting more like Piggy, but that does not necessarily mean he is weak.)

Jack sounds childish when he says that Ralph "isn't a prefect," meaning he hasn't been given authority over the others by some adult. He accuses Ralph of giving orders he wants obeyed. Again Jack is correct about Ralph, but he lacks the human compassion that Ralph has developed.

When Jack again loses the boys' vote on the leadership, he begins to cry. We see Jack's desire for power side by side with his immaturity and his inability to understand human relationships. His desire to force himself on the others as leader and his childishness are placed together several times in the story. In doing this, Golding may be hinting that those who seek power in this way are often immature and without understanding of the human situation.

Jack leaves the tribe, and the end of the story begins here with Jack's decision.

Piggy is glad Jack is gone, and Simon continues the discussion about the beast. He suggests they climb the mountain to find out whether there really is a beast. The boys react with terror; even Piggy doesn't understand what good it will do. Simon says, "What else is there to do?"—implying that the only way not to fear the beast is to face it. Simon's final journey begins and ends with that question.

Piggy suggests they build a fire on the beach, away from the beast. We watch his stature emerging; with Jack gone, Piggy is able to think and to contribute to the group. Civilization functions well when the threat of savagery is removed.

But the effort to keep the fire going is too much, as it has always been, and the boys slip away into the jungle. Piggy insists they can do all right, but Ralph is not sure. He is aware that Simon is missing.

In a brief scene we follow Simon up the mountain. He is the pilgrim or prophet type, like a Jesus or a Moses, who goes off alone to pray. He meditates, surrounded by dancing butterflies and threatening heat. This combination of beauty and menace will appear again; it is the key to understanding Simon's vision.

The scene shifts to Jack, who is "looking brilliantly happy." Once the leader of a choir, Jack is now self-appointed chief. The choirboys still have remnants of their black caps, but when Golding recalls that "their voices had been the song of angels," he convinces us they have become devils.

Jack has plans. He will be chief, and they will hunt. "Forget the beast," he tells them. If they can forget to think about the beast—if they can forget to think— they can cease to be human, cease to make choices. They can forget the beast by becoming it. Jack also plans to lure the other boys away from Ralph; he will manipulate them, and he will leave an offering for the beast in the hope that the beast will be pacified and manipulated too.

The hunt begins and we travel through the pig runs with the boys. Golding does not spare the reader the details of the killing. We see Jack at the full height of his powers. His regression to an animalistic state thrills the other hunters.

The description of the stalking and the killing of the pig is filled with sexual references. The sow is seen first with her piglets, a cruel commentary on the boys' choice. The hunters, "wedded to her in lust," throw themselves on her. Like someone being raped, the sow "squealed and bucked and the air was full of sweat and noise and blood and terror." Roger unleashes the final cruelty by shoving his spear deep inside the pig. "Right up her ass!" he brags. In this society created by the hunters, there is neither order nor choice; there is only power over others, the force of one's own will pitted against another living creature.

Jack, pleased with his mastery, rubs pig blood on Maurice. It is a baptism in which they have all taken part. Jack talks easily as he cuts up the pig, making plans for a feast, giving orders for a stick to be sharpened at both ends. Then all are silenced as the pig's head is mounted on the stick as a gift for the beast. "The silence accepted the gift." The boys leave quickly. They have honored the beast, and the presence of evil—theirs or the beast's—is all too real. Their action takes on proportions too big and too irrational to contemplate.

Throughout the description of the slaughter, the ironic detail of the butterflies dancing overhead served to remind us of two things: Ralph's conclusions about the indifference of nature and the presence of Simon. Simon is nearby and has watched the massacre.

Like many another prophet in the wilderness, Simon contemplates a vision. His vision is of the pig's head. At first he tires to convince himself that the boys have only been playing a game ("It was a joke really"). The boys' actions throughout have been partly games; can't this be just one more game they've been playing? But nature presses on him and the butterflies disappear. Flies swarm around the pig's guts and around Simon. An equation is drawn: The flies on the pig's head represent the forces of evil in nature, and the flies on Simon represent the forces of evil within. "That ancient, inescapable recognition" of evil within man brings on his seizure.

Meanwhile, Piggy and Ralph are fumbling to understand the fear which is overtaking the island. Their only hope is the fire, "a rope when you were drowning," Ralph says, or medicine when you were sick. But Ralph can't make the boys see it that way. When Ralph asks Piggy, "What's wrong? . . . What makes things break up like they do?" Piggy blames Jack.

Neither of them can see the whole problem. Each wants to believe in some kind of blind idea. Piggy thinks that if Jack and people like him were not around, it might be all right. Ralph, who had strong beliefs, is now confused; he wants to retain his beliefs but is unable to do so.

Have you ever been told something which made no sense to you? Perhaps you dismissed it or forgot it because you had no place to store the information. That's their situation; Ralph and Piggy are stumbling through a jungle of the mind, trying to understand ideas that are not clear to them and make no sense in terms of what they know of civilized man. Neither of them can see or accept what Simon comes to know on the mountain. Piggy believes that other people might have badness in them but that he does not, even though he participated in the murder. Ralph is baffled, unable to understand why common sense doesn't work on the island. It doesn't work because man is partly irrational; without civilization to guide him, man reverts to a primitive nature. This reasoning is too difficult for Ralph to comprehend.

When Jack appears, naked except for his mask, they mistake him for the beast. Jack is now addressed as "Chief," which indicates a loss of name and personal identity. He invites them to the feast.

Ralph tries to hold an assembly with the few remaining boys. He speaks of the importance of the fire over the feast, but "a shutter . . . flickered in his brain," and he loses his train of thought. His self-doubt and the loss of his role as leader cause Ralph to lose his grip on reality. It's as if his mind wants to sink into the void so that he no longer has to be human and can exist mindlessly, like an animal. The little ones want to have fun, and Ralph can't convince them not to go. Thunder seems to announce the coming tragedy.

The final scene of the chapter is Simon's. He is talking with the mounted pig's head, now called the Lord of the Flies. That title is a translation of the word Beelzebub, another name for the devil. Here is the very core of the story and the answer to Ralph's question about why things break down.

The Lord of the Flies says to Simon, "You knew, didn't you? I'm part of you? Close, close, close! I'm the reason why it's no go? Why things are what they are?" What Simon realizes is that evil does not exist outside man's nature. There is no beast in the jungle; evil comes from within man's heart. We ourselves generate the evil in the world. We are what's in the jungle.

No one else, not Ralph or Piggy or Jack, sees the full picture. Each for his own reasons cannot understand the true nature of evil. And the Lord of the Flies warns Simon not to bother telling them because they will never understand.

Simon battles mentally with the Lord of the Flies and refuses to be persuaded by his tactics. "Pig's head on a stick," he says. Because Simon refuses not to tell the truth, he will die a hero.

"We are going to have fun on this island," the head says, ironically echoing Ralph's words when they first landed. Simon looks into the vast mouth of the pig. "There was blackness within, a blackness that spread." Again there is the equation of evil, darkness, and the unknown within and without.

The Lord of the Flies' final words echo Ralph's words when he struck the boar and experienced the thrill of hunting. "We shall do you. See? Jack and Roger and Maurice and Robert and Bill and Piggy and Ralph." The Lord of the Flies names them all and foretells Simon's inevitable end.

CHAPTER NINE

Simon sees the beast that the boys fear. Ralph and Piggy eat pig meat, then join the circle to dance. Simon, mistaken for the beast, is murdered and his body carried away by the ocean waves.

Nature is deadly calm, waiting for the storm to arrive. Only "the flies who blackened their lord and made the spilt guts look like a heap of glistening coal" are moving. The description of nature is vile: "When the creepers shook the flies exploded from the guts with a vicious note and clamped back on again."

Simon awakens from his trance knowing he must tell the others that evil lurks within each of them. Like the prophet who has had his vision, he must return with the truth. Simon staggers from exhaustion and the weight of the message he carries.

Recall how the times of day have been described to correspond with phases in the aging process. Simon, now "like an old man," is free from confusion about life; his vision has freed him but left him old, as at the end of the day. And evening is drawing near.

When Simon sees the dead parachutist covered with flies, he understands that the beast they feared is nothing but a rotting body. The sight sickens him, but Simon frees the corpse from the tangle of strings that had manipulated it.

On the beach Piggy and Ralph are talking. The others have gone to join the feast—"Just for some meat," Piggy says, but Ralph adds that they've gone to hunt and put on war-paint too. Ralph knows they seek the protection and power they feel in hunting as a tribe.

When Ralph and Piggy join the party, they find Jack enthroned. "Jack, painted and garlanded, sat there like an idol. There were piles of meat on green leaves near him, and fruit, and coconut shells full of drink." As chief, he offers them "the gift" of meat. There is subtle irony here, for the gift is more like a poison; those who eat will be contaminated and will participate in killing. Simon, the only boy who hasn't eaten, will be killed.

Jack rules very differently than Ralph did. Where Ralph tried to hold assemblies in which each could speak and all were respected, Jack rules by fear and force, shouting commands that always contain a threat. "Power lay in the brown swell of his forearms: authority sat on his shoulder and chattered in his ear like an ape." Jack's power resides in his ability to bully others, and this power has gone to his head.

The struggle to be leader surfaces again between Jack and Ralph. "Who'll join my tribe and have fun?" Jack shouts. The thunder overhead frightens the littl-uns. "Where are your shelters?" Ralph asks, making the hunters stop and think.

Ralph comes close to convincing them to follow him, as they have done so many times. But Jack is more conniving now, and when he realizes he is about to lose to Ralph, he acts. "Do our dance! Come on! Dance!" he yells and leads the boys into their rit-ual as lightning begins to flash.

Nature has gone mad and Piggy and Ralph, now poisoned, join the circle. They "found themselves eager to take a place in this demented but partly secure society. They were glad to touch the brown backs of the fence that hemmed in the terror and made it governable." The two boys fear the isolation of staying outside the circle, of being alone with the elements. By joining the savage circle and letting go of his individuality, neither will have to think about the beast in nature.

"Kill the beast! Cut his throat! Spill his blood!" The chant has turned from pig to beast, an indication of the power they place in the ritual. The chant carries them into a mindless frenzy. They cease to be scared little boys afraid of the dark and become a mob with-out conscience, gaining power and security through chant and ritual. As if nature were rousing them to an even more heightened frenzy, the sky is cut by light-ning and "the noise was on them like the blow of a gigantic whip." Nature, like a devil or a beast, cracks it over the boys.

The mob seeks the pure thrill of killing. "Out of the terror rose another desire, thick, urgent, blind." The boys can deal with their fear of a beast more powerful than they are only by turning their terror against a creature weaker than they are. This is what Jack has done to Piggy throughout the story; it is what he has taught the boys.

A "thing" crawls out of the jungle, and they seize on it. "The beast was on its knees in the center, its arms folded over its face. It was crying out . . . about a body on the hill." The beast is Simon and the boys kill him with their sticks.

Immediately the rain begins to fall, and as the boys scatter they "see how small a beast it was." Once the lust for blood has been satisfied, madness recedes and conscience returns. And nature sends down fresh, cool rain that is like a cleansing.

Simon is approached by waves streaked with "moonbeam-bodied creatures with fiery eyes." In the book's most lyrical and most beautiful passage, nature seems to pay tribute to Simon. He is carried out to sea, his coarse hair "dressed . . . with brightness. The line of his cheek silvered and the turn of his shoulder became sculptured marble." As the creatures carry him off, Simon's mouth emits an ugly bubble, a gasp that reminds us that a murder has taken place and that nature doesn't really care about man.

The point of view, which has been very close to the earth, the boys' fear, Simon's murder, now pulls back. "Somewhere over the darkened curve of the world the sun and moon were pulling." Simon is being pulled out to sea in a graceful sweep of ocean waves, but Simon is also dead. There is both beauty and ugliness in the world. Both are a part of existence;

one cannot be denied for the other. Both are there, both are necessary. This is life and this is what Simon understood that no one else on the island can come to terms with.

CHAPTER TEN

The boys cope in different ways with Simon's murder, Ralph and Piggy at one end of the island, Jack and the hunters at the other. During the night Jack steals Piggy's glasses.

Piggy and Ralph are both described as having faulty vision—a symbolical indication of their limited understanding of the beast. Ralph's eye is swollen shut, and Piggy, though he is seeing a little better, is still nearly blind. They try to discuss what was done to Simon. "What are we going to do?" Ralph asks. They are very much equals now, and Ralph laughs when Piggy reminds him he's still chief. Being chief and having the conch no longer have meaning. And they've committed murder. Ralph's conscience is deeply troubled because he can't understand what happened. In the darkness of the night he responded to his fears, and now that it's light he cannot explain how or why he did what he did. "I was—I don't know what I was."

Piggy can't listen to Ralph's words. " 'It wasn't—what you said.' He was gesticulating, searching for a formula." Piggy can't even use the word "murder," as though not saying it will somehow undo what has happened. Piggy makes excuses, looking for a way to dismiss or rationalize what he's done. In the civilized world of adults that Piggy has tried to keep alive, these things don't happen. Or when they do, murder is committed by bad people, people who are different, not by good, sane people like himself. This is the formula Piggy is trying to find, but the fact that he participated in the murder has already proven it false.

Piggy's argument says that these things don't take place where there are civilized societies. Yet the boys are on the island because the world has just seen an atomic war. And when you consider the rise of Hitler and the barbarities of the concentration camps, you know that civilized people do commit murder. This is the dreadful truth that Simon found, that people are both good and evil.

When the twins appear, no one can admit to what has been done, and the boys are embarrassed in front of one another. Ralph, Piggy, and Samneric are incapable of saying, I murdered; I am a murderer. They cannot name what they've done.

Recall the idea of naming and the power of something that has no name. The same idea applies to admitting the truth. To tell the truth is to call something by its true name. Can you remember doing something you wanted no one to know about? Did you find yourself worrying that someone might find out your secret? On the other hand, when you admit to something you've done wrong, your trouble seems to go away. You forget about it after awhile; it no longer has power over your mind.

This is the problem the boys are struggling with. Telling the truth about what they've done to Simon is painful and has dire consequences.

Meanwhile, at their end of the island, the hunters are also dealing with the murder. To protect themselves from anything that might try to harm them, they post a guard. Robert shows Roger the massive rock with the lever under it, which can be hurled down if the beast appears.

They talk about the chief—no longer Jack, their "friend," but their leader. When Roger hears that the chief is going to beat Wilfred without offering an explanation for the beating, he realizes that the civilization which had protected the littluns is gone. He "sat still, assimilating the possibilities of irresponsible authority." Roger is Jack's right-hand man, much as Piggy is Ralph's. As Jack does, Roger understands the use of force and enjoys it. He is linked with rocks, a brute force, throughout the story. At the beginning, he can't throw them; here, he is sitting on a large rock when he realizes that he can do whatever he wants and no one will stop him. Roger will be responsible for freeing the rock which kills Piggy.

The boys sit around the chief like a group of slaves or dogs. No one thinks to question Wilfred's beating. The chief gives the orders. When one of the boys has something to say, the chief condescends to listen. The only one who knows anything is the chief; the boys ask questions, the chief has the answers. This is a far different assembly from Ralph's.

Jack is equated now with evil. His tongue is like a snake's: The boys see "a triangle of startling pink dart out, pass along his lips and vanish." Jack uses his sinister powers to keep the boys in line. He terrifies them by bringing up their own fears: "The beast might try to come in. You remember how he crawled—" This society is based on fear and manipulation.

The hunters believe they have killed the beast, but Jacks says, "No! How could we—kill—it?" There's no way to kill a beast that could be anywhere, could be anything. And if the beast disguises itself, there would be no end to the terror.

Jack uses the boys' fear of the beast to suit his own

purposes. When he wants the boys shaken by fear, he twists his words to create terror. And when he wants to travel through the jungle after dark in spite of the terror, he dismisses the protests with condescension.

Piggy and Ralph light a fire to serve a "double function": They need it as a signal and also for comfort against the dark. Eric asks if there's any purpose in keeping a fire going. Ralph tries to answer convincingly, but "that curtain flapped in his head and he forgot what he had been driving at."

The void which Ralph doesn't want to feel—the sense of nature's indifference to man, the fact that rescue may not come, the beast, the unknown—all his fears push forward in his mind, causing his old beliefs to waver. He gives in, letting go, "feeling curiously defenseless with the darkness pressing in." The darkness in his mind and the fears of the night gather around him. The boys let the fire die.

In the shelter, Ralph lulls himself to sleep with a tame fantasy; the jungle is no longer an "attractive" daydream. When Piggy awakens him, they listen "to something moving outside." In a moment that is at once painfully funny, true to life, and horrible, Piggy hears his name being called. Outside the shelter could be the beast or the ghost of Simon. Fear brings on an asthma attack, and a battle begins in total darkness.

"We've had a fight with the others," Ralph calls out to the littluns when it's over. There is yet another touch of irony here: Jack has attacked Ralph's shelters, but in the darkness Ralph, Piggy, and the twins have mostly beaten up each other.

"I thought they wanted the conch," Piggy says. But Jack knows the conch is useless. They've taken Piggy's glasses, the one tool Jack lacked for building a fire. The loss of his sight makes Piggy's death inevitable. We don't know how, but we know it has to be. The loss of the glasses spells the end of any kind of order or sanity on the island.

The last paragraph of the chapter describes the hunters, Jack among them, turning cartwheels on the beach. In a sad and ironic way, their action mirrors the beginning of the book.

CHAPTER ELEVEN

Ralph and Piggy cross the island to get the glasses back. A huge rock is set free by Roger, killing Piggy and shattering the shell. Ralph flees for his life.

In the morning the fire has died, and without Piggy's glasses the boys have no way to relight it. Again Ralph asks the question, "Are we savages?" It seems to him incredible that they could not keep a simple fire going to insure their rescue. He blames Jack once more, but no one is really to blame; the problem is their inability to understand human nature. He suggests they talk with the other tribe.

Before he speaks, Piggy takes the conch, still following the practices of civilization. He calls for action; he wants his glasses back. Yet Piggy recognizes that his situation is hopeless. "You can take spears if you want but I shan't. . . . I'll have to be led like a dog, anyhow."

Ralph protests, "You'll get hurt."

"What can he do more than he has?" Piggy replies, knowing he's lost without his glasses. Piggy, who has been the brunt of ridicule, who is physically weak, now begins to show his real strength. Our impression of him changes as he talks. He defends what he believes. He wants to go to Jack and say, "I don't ask for my glasses back, not as a favor. I don't ask you to be a sport . . . not because you're strong, but because what's right's right." Piggy understands fairness and decency, which of course Jack doesn't.

Piggy's effort is doomed, but because he persists he becomes a tragic hero, one who carries on in spite of what awaits him. "Piggy sought in his mind for words to convey his passionate willingness to carry the conch against all odds."

The twins, the only other boys who remain with Ralph, want to paint themselves like the hunters, but Ralph refuses to allow it.

They are a sorry crew crossing the island. Both Ralph and Piggy have problems with their sight; they are like the blind leading the blind. They pass the place where Simon was killed, but nature has washed away all signs of that violence. Ralph looks at different spots and thinks of what took place in each one. His mind is like that of an old man, reflecting over a lifetime. The procession he leads is like a funeral procession.

They arrive at Castle Rock, Jack's fort. Piggy waits at the edge of the cliff, a person on the brink of death. He asks, "Am I safe? I feel awful—" What awaits him is awful. Golding's tragic hero feels terror on the brink of what he is about to do.

Ralph goes forward with his own personal inability to fathom what he is dealing with in the hunters. Warned to halt, he responds in an adult way, "Stop being silly!" Ralph no longer sees the game in what they are doing.

Piggy urges, "Don't leave me, Ralph." On this end of the island, in the face of Jack's reign of terror, Piggy's nobility appears painfully absurd.

Ralph's hard-won compassion comes through. He tells Piggy, "Kneel down and wait till I come back." This is a sensitive Ralph, a Ralph very different from the boy who once thoughtlessly revealed Piggy's name. But this is also the same Ralph in many respects, for he still doesn't understand how vulnerable Piggy really is.

Above them, Roger is flinging stones. There is something obscene about his aiming to miss, as though he were counting the seconds until he can satisfy his lust for violence. "Some source of power began to pulse in Roger's body."

Suddenly Jack appears with a gutted pig, and Piggy wails, "Ralph! Don't leave me!" Together, Piggy's plea and the sow's body seem to comment on each other; by implication, Piggy is a dead pig. The tension becomes unbearable.

Ralph accuses Jack of being a thief, and he has more than the glasses in mind. Jack has stolen the fire, the leadership, and the tribe. The fight we've been waiting for finally breaks out, then halts momentarily at Piggy's reminder of why they've come.

Ralph speaks, but again Jack creates a diversion to draw attention away from him. The twins are seized and sucked into the savagery of brute force and the use of fear. "See?" Jack says, "they do what I want." Jack's words carry many meanings: He is letting Ralph know how to be a ruler, telling Ralph that he can and does rule better, pointing out that Ralph has failed.

Ralph responds to the goading, and this is exactly what Jack wants. If Jack can get Ralph enraged, he can bring about the showdown between them. Jack will not rest until the threat to his leadership is destroyed.

Ralph, pushed to his limits, without taking time to think, shouts. "You're a beast and a swine and a bloody, bloody thief!" And Jack, "knowing this was the crisis," throws himself into battle with Ralph.

Again Piggy halts the fight by demanding to speak. "I got the conch!" The boys boo—the conch means nothing in Jack's world, for the right to speak has been destroyed—but they listen out of curiosity. Overhead, Roger throws stones while toying maliciously with the lever under the gigantic rock. He sees Ralph as "a shock of hair" and Piggy as "a bag of fat."

In a last noble attempt to show the worth of civilization, Piggy asks a series of questions. "Which is better—to be a pack of painted Indians . . . or to be sensible . . . ? Which is better—to have rules and agree, or to hunt and kill? Which is better, law and rescue, or hunting and breaking things up?" But these are the questions the boys have been unable to come to terms with all along.

Piggy gets his answer. "High overhead, Roger, with a sense of delirious abandonment, leaned all his weight on the lever." Brute force is better. Might makes right whatever it wants.

The rock shatters the shell and hurls Piggy to his death on the rocks below. On Jack's side of the island we see the boy's death like the death of a pig. "Piggy's arms and legs twitched a bit, like a pig's after it has been killed." In this world there is no understanding of nobility or heroism.

Without a bit of remorse for what's just happened and as if to prove that he has no understanding, Jack turns on Ralph and threatens him with the same kind of death. "The conch is gone . . . I'm chief." Jack asserts the only thing that is important to him—power.

Ralph flees, obeying "an instinct that he did not know he possessed." Now that sanity and order have been destroyed with Piggy and the shell, Jack's rule will be unchallenged. Everyone else, including Ralph, will be reduced to surviving by animal instinct alone.

CHAPTER TWELVE

The novel that began with the noble summons of the shell ends with the cry of savages.

Ralph escapes into the jungle. He is now the beast pursued, and he has no time to clean his wounds. Like an animal, he must remain constantly alert.

Seeing one of the boys, Ralph thinks, "This was not Bill. This was a savage whose image refused to blend with that ancient picture of a boy in shorts and shirts." The civilized world they came from is completely gone; they exist now in a world of their own making. We readers are so caught up in Ralph's plight that our awareness of the outside world is also gone. We follow Ralph closely, experiencing his isolation and his being stalked.

At first Ralph tries to convince himself that the boys won't harm him, that they might only make him an "outlaw." But he can't make himself believe they'll let him be a Robin Hood in the jungle. "Fatal unreasoning knowledge" of what has been done to Simon and Piggy cannot be dismissed. "These painted savages would go further and further," Ralph knows, and they won't stop until they've gotten him too. He is a threat, and that is the "indefinable connection between himself and Jack"; Jack cannot abide a threat to his throne.

Ralph returns to Jack's side of the island, hoping that in daylight he can reason with the boys. He comes upon the pig's head, now a skull resting on a stick. He recognizes it as a talisman but a more sinister one than the conch. The Lord of the Flies does not speak to Ralph as it did to Simon, but something of its evil nature "prickles" at the edges of Ralph's understanding. "A sick fear and rage swept him," and Ralph lashes out at the skull. Ralph will never understand what Simon learned on the mountain. His fear causes him to break the skull, and he takes the stick the skull was mounted on.

Feeling bitterly alone, Ralph tries to pretend they are "still boys, schoolboys." But he knows that even if he could believe it by day, he couldn't at night. He has become "an outcast," the beast, the thing Jack will hunt.

Just when he thinks nothing more can happen, Ralph discovers new wounds. Samneric have joined the tribe and are "guarding the Castle Rock against him." Even though he knows there is no hope, Ralph sneaks up to talk to them. They tell him about the hunt Jack is planning in order to catch him. When Ralph wonders why it has to be, Eric says, "Listen, Ralph. Never mind what's sense. That's gone—"

Indeed, all sense has gone out of the world. No one but Ralph bothers to think any longer, and that's why he's in trouble. "They're going to do you," the twins tell him. This is the same phrase that Ralph used about the sow and that the Lord of the Flies spoke to Simon. We equate it with death.

The final news is that Roger has "sharpened a stick at both ends." Ralph can't make sense out of that, but it strikes dread in him. Roger had abused the dying pig by thrusting a spear inside her; her head was mounted on such a stick; and Roger used a stick to free the boulder that killed Piggy. Ralph wonders what horror Roger has planned for him.

Ralph feels Piggy's presence and the terrible memory of his death. If Piggy's ghost were to return, its brains would be bashed out because of the way he died. He would be the beast. The jungle offers Ralph little comfort, and he sleeps near the tribe who will hunt him in the morning. Little is left of Ralph's rational mind when he falls asleep.

He awakens with a start. "The age-long nightmares of falling and death were past and . . . the morning was come. Ralph's real death is about to begin.

Ralph hears the twins betray his hideout and prepares himself for battle. He realizes that he will kill or be killed if someone tries to enter the thicket in which he hides. Instead the savages heave a boulder at him, and he is thrust out by its impact. Then they set fire to his hiding place. He is chased through the jungle, stalked and hunted down like a pig.

His thinking ability has diminished, but Ralph is still thinking. He tries to decide between climbing a tree, where he may or may not be spotted, and rushing their lines like the boar did. It's a terrible choice. "The tree, or the charge?" he asks himself, attempting to decide like a human being. "Think," he tells himself again and again, trying to resist "the curtain that might waver in his brain, blacking out the sense of danger, making a simpleton of him."

He decides to hide and wonders "if a pig would agree." Ralph grimaces, but he's now a hunted creature himself. The burning jungle which surrounds him begins to merge with the chaos in his mind.

"Now the fire was nearer; those volleying shots were great limbs, trunks even, bursting." Ralph is in the hell that Piggy saw coming because they were not acting civilized. In his hiding place, Ralph realizes that the stick he's been carrying is "sharpened at both ends," and he understands what will happen to his head when Jack captures him. The savages are only a little distance from him. Ralph tells himself, "Don't scream. Get ready."

A savage looks into Ralph's hiding place and sees "a blob of dark." (Remember that the conch was called a blob and Piggy was considered a blob.) Ralph, linked now to what has been destroyed, tries to remain calm. "Don't scream. You'll get back. Now he's seen you. He's making sure. A stick sharpened." The short words, the brief sentences make our breath quicken, and we feel Ralph's anxiety.

He thinks only on a primitive level now; he's no longer capable of more than basic notions. "You'll get back," a reference to Simon's prophesy, is the only hopeful note in the chapter.

Then Ralph screams, and the scream is a trapped animal's death wail. "He shot forward . . . screaming, snarling, bloody." He runs through the burning jungle, a hell of the boys' own making. "He forgot his wounds, his hunger and thirst, and became fear; hopeless fear on flying feet." He has been reduced to a mindless animal whose muscles have taken over. The last shreds of Ralph's humanity are gone as he crashes through the jungle and tumbles onto the beach, "trying to cry for mercy."

The ending of the story takes us by surprise—in fact, we slam into it like a speeding train hitting a brick wall. There on the beach stands a naval officer in a white uniform. We stop with Ralph to catch our breath.

Golding turns us around and shows us the boys as the officer must see them, "little boys, their bodies streaked with colored clay, sharp sticks in their hands." The abrupt shift in perspective reminds us that these little boys have seduced themselves into a deadly game.

"Fun and games," the officer observes. "Having a war or something?" But it's not a game; what they've been doing is serious. Ralph understands this, and Golding has been trying to convince us of it by allowing us to be so close to Ralph.

"We'll take you off," the officer says. "Who's boss here?"

Ralph can answer "I am" now that civilization has returned. Jack is described as "a little boy who wore the remains of an extraordinary black cap on his red hair and who carried the remains of a pair of spectacles at his waist." He begins to protest, then changes his mind. It would seem that Jack's rule is over.

The officer thinks the boys could have done better in conducting themselves on the island. Ironically, he repeats the same childish view that the boys had when they landed. Ralph, unable to speak, can only weep for "the end of innocence, the darkness of man's heart, and the fall through the air of the true, wise friend called Piggy."

The last paragraph is the most chilling. Ralph and the boys appear to have been saved and Jack's rule destroyed. Again the perspective shifts, and we look away from the boys and out toward the cruiser. The boys will be heading into another war. Ralph has been saved not to return to the home he has dreamed of but to be carried toward a larger war not of his making. Those who are conducting the war have the same immature attitudes about civilization and power that the boys on the island had. The Jacks of the world may yet have their way.

The dramatic change in perspective moves the focus away from the boys and turns it on the world and on us. Ralph has made war just as men of the world do. Ralph and the boys are like the rest of humanity; even in this ideal place they have bowed to the warring instinct because thinking and choice are so difficult. Golding is telling his readers that we too will be destroyed. We must remember that the world which surrounds us is our island, and we must each feel and act responsibly toward it. We have a responsibility to protect our civilization and its freedoms, especially the freedoms of choice and speech.

A STEP BEYOND

Tests and Answers

TESTS

Test 1

1. Golding's characters, a group of English _____
   schoolboys, find themselves on a tropical
   island as a result of
   A. punishment for criminal behavior
   B. an atomic war
   C. a deliberate escape from civilized society

2. Blown by Piggy, the conch is _____
   A. thrown up on the beach by a sudden
      storm
   B. seized by Jack and blown
   C. a symbol of authority, order, and
      civilization

3. The boys' initial reaction to their new _____
   environment on the island is
   A. fear of the unknown
   B. indifference because they're too young to
      react
   C. joy over a fantasy come true

4. Ralph is characterized as being _____
   A. handsome, athletic, a natural leader
   B. intellectual, a misfit
   C. sensitive, poetic, spiritual

5. "I got the conch. I got the right to speak." _____
   Who is speaking here?
   A. Piggy   B. Simon   C. Ralph

6. The "snake" or scar that cuts across the island   _____
   may suggest
   A. an Indian magician's snake at a bazaar
   B. the atomic war that could have preceded
      the boys' arrival on the island
   C. the snake in Genesis, a reference to the
      corruption and downfall of man

7. There is irony in the words, "We've got to   _____
   have rules and obey them. After all, we're not
   savages." Who is speaking here?
   A. Jack   B. Piggy   C. Ralph

8. Jack is characterized as being   _____
   A. intelligent and sensitive
   B. cruel, a bully, Ralph's chief competitor
   C. poetic, religious, sensitive

9. *Lord of the Flies* is told from the point of view   _____
   of
   A. Piggy
   B. Ralph
   C. the omniscient author

10. "Samneric" refers to   _____
    A. identical twin boys
    B. a green tropical plant used as food
    C. medicine for Piggy's asthma

11. Define *irony* and point out three places where it is used
    in the novel.

12. Compare Ralph's use of power with Jack's use of power.

13. What does the conch symbolize in the novel? How does
    the author make us understand its significance?

14. Piggy's glasses and his limited vision are important in
    the novel. How are they significant, and what theme(s)
    do they represent?

Test 2

1. "We've got to have special people looking after the fire. Any day there may be a ship out there." Who is speaking here? _____
   A. Piggy   B. Ralph   C. Simon

2. Piggy's glasses _____
   A. gave him insight into people's character
   B. were destroyed by Simon
   C. were used to light a fire and may have been a symbol of his intelligence

3. "I don't believe in no ghosts, ever." Who is speaking here? _____
   A. Piggy   B. Sam or Eric   C. Simon

4. The smashing of the sand castles may have represented _____
   A. the passing of the boys' childhood
   B. the "norming" of competitive behavior
   C. the "norming" of violence

5. "The beast that came out of the sea" was _____
   A. a bad dream of the littluns
   B. a downed navy pilot
   C. never determined

6. One important character who is not present when the boys pursue the boar is _____
   A. Piggy   B. Roger   C. Simon

7. The evil behavior that emerges in many of the boys as the novel evolves is reminiscent of what takes place in _____
   A. Hemingway's *For Whom the Bell Tolls*
   B. Conrad's *Heart of Darkness*
   C. Steinbeck's *Of Mice and Men*

8. According to Golding, the title *Lord of the Flies* _____
   A. refers to the boys as "lords" of the island
   B. has significance for scholars only
   C. is the literal Hebrew translation of "Beelzebub"

9. "Kill the pig. Cut her throat. Bash her in." _____
   Who is speaking here?
   A. All the hunters   B. Jack
   C. Ralph

10. Simon is characterized as being _____
   A. loyal, poetic, sensitive
   B. a leader, competitive, fair-minded
   C. intelligent and intellectual

11. How does Golding let the reader know in Chapter 1 that the island, which the boys believe is a paradise, is a dangerous place?

12. Why do the boys believe in the natural goodness of man?

13. What is the importance of names, naming, and the loss of names in the story?

14. Give three examples of Jack's becoming more primitive and animalistic.

ANSWERS

Test 1

1. B   **2.** C   **3.** C   **4.** A   **5.** A   **6.** C
7. A   **8.** B   **9.** C   **10.** A

   11. The word *irony* has several meanings. After you have found its definition in an ordinary dictionary, you will want to look it up again in a dictionary of literary terms, which will tell you more about the use of irony in literature. The definition of *irony* that most concerns us here is the use of words to convey meaning that is different from (and usually the exact opposite of) what those words mean literally. For example, someone who hates war might say to you, "War is wonderful!"—but in such a tone of voice that you understand exactly what the person really thinks.

There is irony throughout *Lord of the Flies*. The author uses it in his narrative, the characters are aware of it and use it in their speech, and the events of the story, in relation to one another, are ironic.

At the beginning of the novel, Ralph says that the boys will have a good time on the island until the grownups rescue them. In light of everything that happens on the island (the boys have a horrible time and some of them are even killed), Ralph's words are ironic, even though he does not intend them to be.

Simon is the only one who understands that their fundamental problem is the beast each one carries within himself. Therefore it is ironic that Simon, the intelligent one, cannot speak before the group and is thought "batty" even by Ralph and Piggy. He has no one's respect, and he wants to tell them something that is beyond their understanding.

At the end of the story, the officer thinks the boys "would have been able to put up a better show." The boys once thought so, too; now their experience has made them far more mature than the officer, whose viewpoint is close to that of the boys when they arrived on the island. The officer may also intend another irony in his words, for he speaks of how the boys might have behaved when he knows from what he sees around him that somehow that behavior was not possible.

12. Ralph is elected freely. When he calls the boys together, he tries to be fair by making reasonable rules. He says that each boy will be allowed to speak when he holds the conch and that he can't be interrupted by anyone except himself as their leader. He assigns the important tasks of hunting and keeping the fire going. He does not punish the

boys when they fail at their tasks but talks to them about their responsibilities.

Jack uses force and fear to rule, having bullied his way into power. He forces the twins to join his tribe by tormenting them. The boys are not allowed to speak freely. They can only ask Jack's opinion and accept his answers. He expects to be treated like a god; the boys must wait on him and do what he wants. When they disobey, they know they will be punished or killed.

13. The conch is a symbol of communication. Its sounding calls the boys out of the jungle, as primitive men who existed in isolation and fear were called together. The conch is also a symbol of order. The conch gathers the boys in a group so that they can become a civilization. It calls them away from animalistic and instinctual tendencies and toward awareness and choice. At first all the boys respect the rules which Ralph establishes to hold meetings. Later, when Ralph's leadership has failed, the boys no longer value the conch. After the conch has been destroyed, they return to a primitive order without thought or choice. Although Jack does lead a tribe, there is no unity among its members, only fear and force.

14. In literature, blindness and the ability to see have always been important themes. In Piggy's case, his glasses are a sign that he sees or knows more than most of the other boys. He is more concerned with maintaining civilization and order on the island. Unlike Ralph, Piggy "sees" what will happen if they don't remain civilized.

The glasses symbolize his ability, but at the same time they indicate he has impaired vision. He knows or sees more than Ralph, but he doesn't see the total problem. In the symbolic sense, Piggy's vision of the jungle is impaired. He will blame Jack—who is only part of the problem—and fail to understand that the beast resides within each of the boys, including him.

Test 2

1. B   **2.** C   **3.** A   **4.** C   **5.** B   **6.** C

7. B   **8.** C   **9.** A   **10.** A

11. The author describes the island with words that give the reader subtle clues to what he thinks about the boys' paradise. An ugly "scar" is smashed into the island where wreckage of the plane that dropped them fell. As Ralph breaks through the creepers (even that word indicates menace), a bird the color of fire and heat sounds a "witch-like cry," as if it were announcing doom. Ralph stands among the "skull-like" coconuts. When Piggy appears he is scratched with thorns. This hardly seems like a friendly place, even though Ralph thinks it will be wonderful.

12. The boys have read such adventure stories as *Treasure Island*, *Coral Island*, *Robinson Crusoe*, and *Swiss Family Robinson*. All these books offer the theory that man is corrupted by living in civilization. The premise of each of them is that if man were placed in a more natural setting, say a deserted island or a paradise, he would revert to his original state of natural goodness. The authors of these books, and many people throughout history, believed that civilization, with all its evils, was a corrupter of man. The boys have never thought to question this idea, but that is what Golding does in the novel. The notion that man was good and civilization bad was so widely held that it was accepted as fact by just about everyone in Europe before World War II. Golding began to question the idea after his war experiences.

13. Names are significant in this novel. The nickname Piggy is connected to the killing and eating of pig and what happens to the character. Ralph's name means "counsel," and Ralph tries to rule his meetings by sharing leadership with the others. Jack means "one who supplants," someone who takes power by force— which is exactly Jack's nature.

Simon's name means "listener," and Simon is the only boy who hears the Lord of the Flies.

Certain boys' names are never told; they are recognized only by their size, as "littluns" or "biguns." Some boys lose their names. The twins come to share only one name between them ("Samneric"), and Jack who becomes "Chief." One boy seems to have forgotten his name at the end. The implication is that these boys have lost their personal identities.

In ancient legends, characters were cautious about revealing their names. A person was believed to have power over another if he knew his real name. Someone who wanted to protect himself against his enemies would make up a name for himself and not reveal his real one. In a symbolic sense, that is why Piggy is upset when Ralph tells his name to everyone. Jack gains power over Piggy by being able to mock his name.

When the boys can no longer call the beast by name, it means that the fear of it has overtaken them and gained power over them. Simon is the exception; he can call the beast by name, and even though he fears it, it never gains power over his spiritual nature.

14. In Chapter 3, Jack teaches himself to stalk a pig. He is described as being down on all fours like a dog and unaware of his discomfort. He learns to track like an animal and to ignore pain in his body the way an animal would. He can see in the dark like an animal. Later Jack smells pig droppings, relearning the sense of smell that human beings lost long ago.

After they roast a pig in Chapter 4, Jack tries to describe the feeling of the hunt. His language is very primitive: "I painted my face—I stole up. Now you eat—all of you—and I—" He can hardly express his thoughts anymore; it is as if he were losing the power to think while his animal instincts are gaining strength.

contact with other people.

Reuseable bedding and clothing can be autocla
the virus. People who come into contact with t
such as laundry handlers, housekeeping, and l
equipment. If a case of smallpox is confirmed,
contaminated materials.

(Medical Management)
No antiviral drug is currently approved by the
smallpox. Recent studies suggest that the antiv
But the drug must be administered intravenous
for the treatment of smallpox would

Term Paper Ideas

1. Trace the symbolism of the conch through the novel, showing how the shell is invested with power and how that power is destroyed.

2. Compare the idea of "man's return to a more natural state" in *Tarzan of the Apes* or *Swiss Family Robinson* with what happens in *Lord of the Flies*.

3. Discuss the uses of nature in the novel, showing how it foreshadows what will happen, how it works against man, how it parallels man's emotional states.

4. Discuss Golding's idea of evil in the "darkness of man's heart."

5. Show how Golding uses irony in *Lord of the Flies*.

6. Follow the boys' loss of civilization and discuss the ways in which Golding lets us know they are becoming more and more savage.

7. Compare Piggy and Simon as doomed heroes.

8. Is the novel ultimately optimistic or pessimistic? Give evidence to support your theory.

9. Consider *Lord of the Flies* as a fable and demonstrate what ideas or beliefs Ralph and Jack represent.

10. Who would you have followed if you were on the island with Ralph and Jack and they were your age? What reasons would you have for believing in one or the other?

11. Trace the changes that occur in the nature of "the beast" throughout the story.

12. Follow the development and breakdown of Ralph's idea of game playing.

13. Trace the disintegration of Jack's speech and the rise of his animalistic abilities.

14. Discuss the use of fire imagery in the novel.

15. Compare the authoritarian and democratic power of Jack and Ralph with situations in our world today.

16. Compare Ralph's coming of age in *Lord of the Flies* with the development of the main character in *A Separate Peace* or *Catcher in the Rye*.

17. Follow the breakdown of Ralph's system of beliefs and show how his thinking changes in the story.

18. Compare Ballantyne's *Coral Island* with *Lord of the Flies* and contrast the differences in the outcome of the two stories.

19. If Golding's story is a fable, it will have a point or a moral. What is the moral in *Lord of the Flies?*

20. Discuss Jack's understanding of fear and the beast and show how he uses his knowledge.

21. Show how Golding makes use of light and dark to convey the deeper meanings of his story.

22. Compare Ralph, Jack, and Simon's journey across the island at the beginning of the novel with Ralph, Jack, and Roger's journey later in the story.

23. Describe the impact *Lord of the Flies* has had on you. How has it changed your thinking?

24. The threat of atomic war is a real one. Compare the thinking of people in power today (pro-nukes and anti-nukes, democrats and autocrats) with Ralph and Jack's attitudes.

25. Consider the power of names, naming, and losing a name in the story. Show how Golding uses these concepts to enhance the meaning of his book.

26. Piggy and Ralph consider that man is essentially good and that evil happens because something is wrong with people. Jack is a primitive person who uses power over

others and believes that forces more powerful than himself must be appeased through ceremony and sacrifice. Simon believes that both good and evil reside within each person. Discuss these three views of man and cite examples of them from the story. Does one of these views seem to represent the author's own outlook?

27. Consider whether you believe the boys could really have committed murder. Show how Golding slowly changes the nature of the boys' game playing so that it becomes something greater than play.

28. Compare our first and last views of Ralph and explain how they differ.

29. Discuss Golding's notion that good intentions often bring about bad results. How do Ralph's good intentions fail? Why do they fail?

30. Compare Chapter 1 and Chapter 12 and discuss the ways in which they are related.

31. Each of the opening chapters has a corresponding later chapter which comments on it. Compare one of the following pairs: Chapters 1 and 6, Chapters 2 and 7, Chapters 3 and 8, Chapters 4 and 9. Discuss how the later chapter enhances what we learned from the earlier chapter.

32. Compare *The Inheritors*, another novel by Golding, with *Lord of the Flies*. Discuss the similarity of ideas and themes in the two books.

33. Examine the influences on Golding's life which led him to write *Lord of the Flies*.

34. Consider the title of each chapter as a key to understanding the major ideas in the novel.

35. Defend Jack's position and his actions on the island.

36. How does Golding prepare us for the murder of Simon so that we accept it when it happens?

Further Reading

CRITICAL WORKS

The following works contain useful chapters on *Lord of the Flies.*

Babb, Howard. *The Novels of William Golding.* Columbus: Ohio State University Press, 1970.

Baker, James R. *William Golding: A Critical Study.* New York: St. Martin's, 1965.

Dick, Bernard F. *William Golding.* Boston: Twayne, 1967.

Hynes, Samuel. *William Golding.* New York: Columbia University Press, 1964.

Kinkead-Weekes, Mark, and Ian Gregor. *William Golding: A Critical Study.* New York: Harcourt, Brace, 1968.

Medcalf, Stephen. *William Golding.* Great Britain: Longmans, 1975.

Oldsey, Bernard, and Stanley Weintraub. *The Art of William Golding.* New York: Harcourt, Brace, 1965.

Spitz, David. "Power and Authority: An Interpretation of Golding's *Lord of the Flies.*" in *The Antioch Review,* Spring 1970, pp. 21–33.

Sternlicht, Sanford. "Song of Innocence and Songs of Experience in *Lord of the Flies* and *The Inheritors.*" in *Midwest Quarterly,* July 1968, pp. 383–390.

Talon, Henri. "Irony in *Lord of the Flies.*" in *Essays in Criticism,* July 1968, pp. 296–309.

AUTHOR'S OTHER WORKS

Poems (1934).

The Inheritors (1955). Novel.

Pincher Martin (1956). Novel.

Sometime, Never: Three tales of imagination (1956).

The Brass Butterfly (1958). Play.

Free Fall (1959). Novel.

"Miss Pulkinhorn" in *Encounter*, August 1960. Story.

"Before the Beginning" in *The Spectator*, May 26, 1961.

"Party of one: Thinking as a hobby" in *Holiday*, August 1961. Essay.

The Spire (1964). Novel.

The Hot Gates and Other Occasional Pieces (1965). Reviews and articles.

The Pyramid (1967). Novel.

The Scorpion God (1971). Three short novels.

Darkness Visible (1979). Novel.

Rites of Passage (1980). Novel.

A Moving Target (1982). Novel.

The Paper Men (1984). Novel.

The Critics

On Irony

Irony breaks out between contrasted scenes somewhat distant from one another, and even as far apart as the beginning and the end of the story. For instance, when we first catch sight of Ralph, he is neat, handsome and laughing. . . . When we last see him he is dirty, in rags and sobbing. He had looked forward to a fine clean game and has lived a sordid, terrible drama. He had anticipated an episode as good as a dream and he has been through a nightmare.

—*Henri Talon, "Irony in*
Lord of the Flies*"*

On Golding's Ironic Use of Ballantyne's *Coral Island*

In *Coral Island*, three English boys called Ralph, Jack and Peterkin are shipwrecked on a tropical island, meet pirates and cannibals, and conquer all adversities with English fortitude. . . . good is defined as being English and Christian and jolly, and . . . evil is unchristian, savage and adult. . . . Golding regards *Coral Island* morality as unrealistic, and therefore not truly moral, and he has used it ironically in his own novel, as a foil for his version of man's moral nature.

—*Samuel Hynes,* William Golding

On Innocence and Experience

Lord of the Flies becomes a tale of the emergence to the conscious level of modern man's carnivorous nature and the catastrophe that must accompany this emergence. . . .

—*Sanford Sternlicht, "Song of*
Innocence and Songs of Experience in
Lord of the Flies *and* The Inheritors*"*

On Metaphor in the Novel

Simon insists on climbing the mountain to find out what it (the beast) is. Against the boys' derision he says, and against the warning of the Lord of the Flies he repeats, "What else is there to do?" His intransigence in climbing the mountain, his insistence on understanding, is a metaphor for what the book itself does. The book dares to name the beast, the evil in man's heart, as the beast.

—*Stephen Medcalf*, William Golding

NOTES

NOTES

NOTES

NOTES

NOTES